TALES OF THE CAMINO

One Pilgrim's Journey to
Santiago de Compostela

William Ross Newland

Tales of the Camino: One Pilgrim's Journey to Santiago de Compostela

Published by Wheatmark®
2030 East Speedway Boulevard, Suite 106
Tucson, Arizona 85719
www.wheatmark.com

ISBN: 978-1-62787-609-4
LCCN: 2018938107

This manuscript has been approved for publication by the CIA's Publications Review Board.

Traveller, the road is only
your footprint, and no more;
traveller, there's no road,
the road is your travelling.

Going becomes the road
and if you look back
you will see a path
none can tread again.

*Caminante, son tus huellas
el camino y nada más;
caminante, no hay camino,
se hace camino al andar.*

*Al andar se hace camino
y al volver la vista atrás
se ve la senda que nunca
se ha de volver a pisar.*

—An excerpt from Antonio Machado's poem "Cantares"

Camino de Santiago
Camino francés

Principado
de Asturias

Galicia

Santiago de Compostela
O Pedrouzo
Arzúa
Palas de Rei
Portomarín
Sarria
Triacastela
O Cebreiro
Vilafranca del Bierzo
Ponferrada
Rabanal del Camino
Astorga
San Martín del Camino
León
Mansilla de las Mulas
El Burgo Ranero
Terradillos de los Templarios
Carrión de los C

Ma r

Castilla y León

PORTUGAL

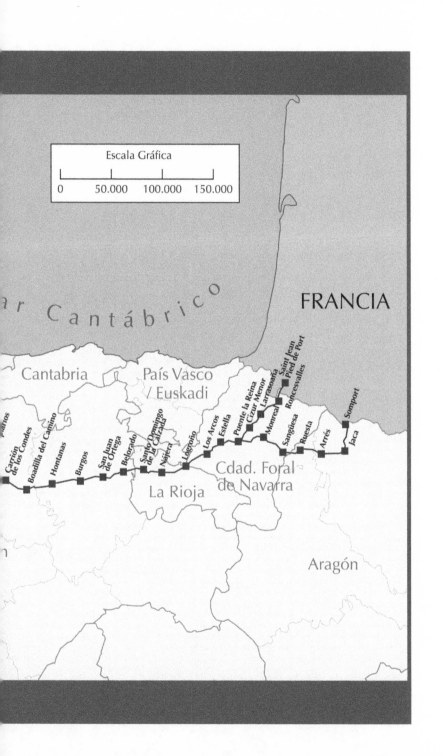

Escala Gráfica

0   50.000   100.000   150.000

mar Cantábrico

FRANCIA

Cantabria

País Vasco / Euskadi

Saint Jean Pied de Port

Larrasaña

Cizur Menor

Puente la Reina

Estella

Los Arcos

Logroño

Nájera

Santo Domingo de la Calzada

Belorado

San Juan de Ortega

Burgos

Hontanas

Boadilla del Camino

Carrión de los Condes

Monreal

Roncesvalles

Sangüesa

Ruesta

Arrés

Jaca

Somport

Cdad. Foral de Navarra

La Rioja

Aragón

PREFACE

Why am I undertaking this journey? Is this just another trip to Spain or is it a mental/philosophical/religious pilgrimage?

Spain is like a former girlfriend to me. I first went to Spain when I was 17 years old, and hitch-hiked and took trains all over the Iberian Peninsula with my best friend. I went back many times, and can speak Spanish like a native. My family moved there once I was back in the U.S. going to university. As a result I visited thirteen times over the next 17 years, sometimes for a week and other times for two months. I have traveled more in Spain than I have in any one country, precisely because I didn't live there. As I was growing up in Mexico, my family traveled there occasionally on vacation, but one's time is consumed by the normal rhythms of growing up: school, work, etc.

I am going to the Camino, literally 'the road,' 'the path,' 'the way,' based on Jesus's statement to his apostles: "I am the way, the truth, and the life." I want to walk on roads that have been walked by a million feet, and add mine to the multitude. I want to think about the fact that each step carried the hopes or prayers or perhaps just the distracted thoughts of millions of pilgrims dating back to the ninth century.

Interest in the pilgrimage to Santiago de Compostela peaked in the 11th–12th centuries, and the first guidebook for pilgrims was the Codex Calixtinus, published in the 12th century. In the past forty years there has been a renewal of interest in the Camino. It is not clear why more people – from all walks of life and from every strata and virtually every country – want to undertake the pilgrimage. It may have something to do with the general loss of interest in formal religion.

I am also eager to look into the history behind the Camino, not just the pilgrims but the places along the way. Burgos and Leon, for example, are full of history. And Santiago itself is as well. The Camino takes the pilgrim though completely different regions of Spain, from the Pyrenees to the Basque Country, Navarre, Castilla, Aragon, and Galicia. Each region has a different culture and cuisine, and each kingdom was originally an independent rival of the others.

In a way I began this journey, this pilgrimage, back in 1976 on my first trip to Spain. Years of travel, work, and raising a family intervened, and now I am back, much older and hopefully a little wiser. The pathway getting here may seem erratic, but I was always bewitched by Spain. I knew I would end up here.

The symbol of the Camino is the scallop shell. It used to be that upon completion of the Camino the pilgrim would be given the shell, in recognition that all roads – like the lines on the shell – lead to Santiago.

I had visited the peninsula more than twenty times over as many years. I knew Madrid, and was enchanted starting many years ago by Cordoba and the Moorish influence in Andalucía. I consider Sevilla one of the most beautiful cities in the world, and the Basque Country and Catalonia have wonderful, rich cultures all their own.

But the Camino would take me to a part of Spain I didn't know. Aside from the cities of Burgos, Leon, and Santiago, the numerous other towns along the Camino stretching from the Pyrenees west across the width of Spain to Santiago are medieval hamlets. They are small, mostly deserted, but rich in Roman history, and in the history of the Reconquest, a 400-year effort to push the Moors out of Spain.

Charlemagne battled the Moors in this region, and in Aragon and Navarra, where the Camino begins. The Camino extends through Castille and Leon, independent kingdoms united by Ferdinand (Castille) and Isabella (Aragon) in 1492 to finally expel the Moors from their last refuge in Granada.

As a result, the area surrounding the Camino is populated by many castles and even more churches. Kings of Castille and Leon built them along battle lines during the Reconquest. The Camino I decided to take extends from Asturias through the great warrior El Cid's birthplace near Burgos, all the way west to Santiago, where St. James' bones were found, near the present-day town of Padron. His remains were transferred to Compostela, thus giving it its modern name, Santiago de Compostela. It was St. James whose figure appeared in an apparition mounted on horseback, depicted as Santiago Matamoros (St. James the Moor slayer), that inspired the Reconquest. Thus in many ways the Camino reflects the history of Roman Spain, of the Reconquest, of El Cid, and Knights Templars.

The Camino also reflects each person's intentions, be they religious or deeply personal, of lost loves and relatives, of hopes and prayers for renewal or thanks.

I want to hear my footsteps on the flagstones and pathways of the Camino, walk where millions have walked before me, see the palaces and the cathedrals, and hear the locals tell stories.

As a lifelong epicure, I want to taste their distinctive food. In the end I will leave my burdens in the form of a rock on a giant medieval pile of rocks, and get on with my life.

And I will be guided by a scallop shell.

INTRODUCTION

As I walk along, sometimes with another pilgrim and often alone for hours at a time, I am seeing, hearing, tasting, and consuming everything around me. I have read the history and the guidebooks so I can absorb the culture and history. My thoughts wander. I see an old church, maybe Romanesque although it is hard to tell from a distance. That mental snapshot makes me think of other similar churches I have seen along the Camino, impressions from other places and other experiences, which gives the sight of the church some context at least in my mind. I collect unfinished thoughts, mull over words, repeat melodies I hear, and of course I expect to remember most of it, which is unrealistic. Didn't St. Augustine say something along the lines of 'Don't search; stop and look'? Hence my desire to write some of this down.

Most of this is in my head and is either unformed or unremembered, so at best the reader is only getting a partial rendition of what happened or what I choose to relate. There is no linear development, at least there usually isn't; instead, it is usually a smattering of images and thoughts and flavors in my head. Most minds work in this fashion, I believe. I can be looking at the cathedral of Leon and think of Mark Twain and Tariq Ali, or of St. James the 'Moor slayer' himself. I wonder simultaneously if the ham croquette tapa I had for lunch was cooked in oil or lard, and how the new U.S. presidency will turn out.

How do I compare to the medieval pilgrim? The medieval man was probably much more spiritual than I, since he (typically he, not she) sought out religious relics – bones and hair of saints, for example – and journeyed far and wide to venerate them. Devout Christians in the Middle Ages made pilgrimages across Europe, to Rome, to Santiago, and to Jerusalem, among other places. Non-Islamic Spain (over half of Spain was Islamic until 1492) felt a bond with the rest of Christian Europe, so as a result the Camino helped unite Christian worshippers. They became united enough that they undertook a series of Crusades into the Levant to retrieve Christian lands.

In medieval times pilgrims took many months to complete the Camino, and took major personal risks. They did not stop at albergues, the pilgrim hostels, but rather at churches, which are more common and spaced more closely together than albergues. At each stop the few monks had four functions to complete with the pilgrim: one monk each was responsible for his physical wellbeing, his nourishment, his mind, and his soul. So the pilgrim was stripped and washed, cured of any ailment; fed; then participated in prayer sessions and philosophical discussions.

And what about me? The legs of my daily walks are longer than the medieval pilgrim's. And although I have been all over Spain at different times and in very different historical junctures over the past 40 years, this is a part of Spain I have never seen, and which is not typically in tourist brochures. I would never claim to 'know' Spain, since a traveler only absorbs a snapshot in time, and within his/her context and experience, limited by language and circumstances.

In this secular day and age, what kind of person does a pilgrimage? What rational being decides to travel to Spain and avoid its magnificence: the Prado in Madrid, the Alhambra in Granada, and the Sagrada Familia in Barcelona, and instead decide to undertake a pilgrimage that involves walking an average of 15 miles per day carrying one's belongings in a backpack, and sleeping in rooms with bunk beds that accommodate anywhere from 30 to 100 fellow pilgrims shuffling, snoring, and rooting around in their backpacks?

I realized that although I completed the Camino I still have a long way to go on my journey.

PART I:
LOGROÑO TO LEON

❧ THE JOURNEY BEGINS

I have felt the call of the Camino for years, and having one of my sons do it a few years ago, and then a good friend complete it last year, really made me ask myself not why but why shouldn't I do it. I trained for months, walking for a few hours at a time, and during my last couple of weeks before going I walked with my loaded backpack just to get used to the feel.

I had wanted to do a two-week Camino ending in Santiago de Compostela with my daughter, but unfortunately just a couple of weeks prior to departure she injured a tendon in her hand and was unable to go. I decided to press ahead and go by myself, but instead of completing the Camino in Santiago I decided to back track two weeks and do the segment of Logroño to Leon, so that once my daughter was able we could do the original plan, which would be Leon to Santiago.

I flew to Madrid and took a bus four hours north to Logroño. Logroño is the heart of La Rioja, Spain's preeminent wine region. It is also known for the quality of its pintxos (tapas). (Note: in Castilla, i.e. central Spain and southern Spain, the small plates of salads, meats, cheeses and croquets are called tapas. In the north, i.e. Navarra and the Basque Country, they are called pintxos. Another distinction is that a true 'tapa' is complementary, and any bar will have two or three options per day of what they offer as a small plate to accompany your beer or wine order. The word 'tapa' comes from the verb 'tapar,' i.e. to cover. Tapas originally derived their name from needing to cover ('tapar') one's wine glass due to flies, and so a piece of ham (jamon Serrano) or a small brusquetta would do.)

Logroño's pintxos are first class, compared to the rest of Spain. Ornate in design, plentiful in quantity, they are also impressive to look at, as opposed to just a saucer with olives or pickled herring. I had a 'bola de marisco' (ball of shellfish) cooked in a batter and lightly fried into the shape and size of a baseball, with a skewer stick on top holding a piece of jamon Serrano as if it were the sail of a ship. I think in Madrid if I had ordered jamon Serrano I would have received a plate with plenty of thinly sliced fine ham, perhaps with a drizzle of olive oil on top. Period.

The wines were excellent, and even the least expensive were fresh Riojas. One asked for this year's harvest, or aged a year or two ('Reserva') to get a more mature wine.

I arrived in Logroño in early evening and immediately headed for the area of town known for its pintxos, along Calle Laurel. The street has winding blocks with dozens of tapa bars, and is known as the 'senda de elefante,' since if you stop to drink and eat pintxos at enough places you will end up walking on all fours like an elephant.

I stopped at one bar and tried the pintxos and a glass of Rioja. The smell and the flavors brought back fond memories of earlier visits. I took a deep breath; I was back in Spain. I then decided it was important to find my lodgings before dark.

I was headed to the Iglesia de Santiago, which (my guide book claimed) accepted pilgrims on a donation basis. I found the church and couldn't help noticing the sculpture of Santiago (St. James) above the main door, on horseback slaying the Moors. St. James was better known as the inspiration for battle than he was for converting souls.

I walked into the church and there was a Mass going on, which I took as a good omen on my first night of the Camino. I waited until the end and then approached a man who I judged to be a sacristan. He told me they take in pilgrims for the night, and directed me to ring the doorbell around the side of the church. I did so, and an older man opened it, asking me in and inquiring whether I had had any dinner. I told him I had a pintxo early, but no dinner so he asked if I wanted to eat with the pilgrims. Of course! So I went upstairs, left my pack in the huge bunk-bedded room, and entered the dining area and sat down to eat with about 25 fellow pilgrims.

In my first encounter the pilgrims welcomed me and passed along the vegetable soup and bread, and then yogurt for dessert. I listened carefully as they initiated me into the pilgrim language. That language is open, direct, and safe. Strangers feel the bond of another fellow pilgrim who has been called to the Camino, and so little is out of bounds in terms of subjects to discuss. At the same time, however, nobody is interested in names or in what job someone might have back in 'the real world'. Instead, they are interested in why you are undertaking this venture, how your health is, and whether or not you have blisters. How far are did you go today and how far are you thinking of going tomorrow?

I had a friendly Canadian man from Vancouver on my left and a pleasant Irish woman from Cork on my right, and I mined them for information on their Caminos to date. They had both started a few days earlier at St. Jean, the French-Spanish border. I noticed immediately that these pilgrims were open, trusting and friendly.

Our hosts were a Spanish married couple in their 60s who had done the Camino various times and upon retirement decided to become 'hospitalers,' from the ancient Knights Hospitalers, to host pilgrims in Logroño. They explained that after dinner we would all go down into the choir of the ancient church and have a prayer before returning to clean up dinner and lay out coffee, bread, and jam for breakfast.

During the prayer service we divided up a series of prayers by language and depending on our nationalities we read one prayer in English, and then ones in Spanish, German, and

French, to include everyone present. These pilgrim prayers were taken from the Psalms.

Afterwards the hospitaler stamped our credencial (our Camino Passport, which we would need to show when we got to Santiago), and we returned upstairs to clean up and set up breakfast.

I then returned to my bunk bed around 9:30 pm to find that most of the pilgrims were already asleep. I unpacked what I needed in the dark and slept well, since I had not had much rest on the flight the night before.

At 5 am people rummaging around and getting up to use the bathroom woke me up. Pilgrims were already packing up and leaving. Having no alternative I did the same, grabbing a coffee upstairs and a piece of toast. I was later to learn that this experience was normal, i.e. in albergues like this one everyone tends to go to sleep early, wake up early, and get an early start on the day's walk. Also, in most albergues they turn on the lights by 7am and want everyone out by 8.

Unlike other albergues I was to experience, this one arranged for coffee and a bite; most did not and there are no bars or cafes open at 5 or 6 am, so for the rest of the Camino you get up and walk an hour or two before finding a place to stop for coffee and a portion ('racion') of ham or tortilla or toast.

It was still dark at about 5:30am, and feeling jetlagged, I stumbled out of the church and started my journey. After months of planning and training, I was exhilarated to be back in Spain and finally walking the Camino.

❧ "MY OWN CAMINO"

I know I am a competitive person. I have always loved sports, keep fit, and even in my professional career there was always competition, jockeying for position, competing for choice assignments.

On the Camino, especially during the first phase, I noticed this trait right away. I would see a walker up ahead and subconsciously would step up my pace to pass them. In competitive running races years ago I used to do the same thing: try to get ahead of that next person, and keep doing that one at a time throughout the race.

Competitiveness is counterproductive on the Camino. I learned this the hard way, charging out of the Iglesia Santiago on my first day from Logroño and going almost 20 miles, earning soreness and blisters that would last me the next two weeks. The Camino punishes you. Punishment comes in the form of blisters, ankle and joint ailments, and exhaustion.

In time I learned how to treat the blisters, or rather was shown by other pilgrims the lore of dealing with blisters so one could keep walking without causing infection.

The phrase 'everyone has his Camino' has various meanings: not only does it mean that everyone has his/her intention and experience on the Camino, but one should walk at one's own speed. It is a pilgrimage, not a group exercise or a race.

Some pilgrims went at their own pace, speaking with others when they wished, taking in the beauty of the countryside, letting their mind wander to deep personal and spiritual issues. On the Meseta portion, I thought of the Roman legions, the Knights Templars, and St. Francis of Assisi traveling this same road.

Others didn't seem to 'get it.'

One young Italian woman passed me with her metal hiking poles clicking on the pavement. Although it was late in the afternoon already and I was stopping at the next town, she told me she would push on to one more town since she 'had to' average over 30 kilometers (almost 20 miles) per day. When I mentioned a Romanesque Church from the 12th century in this town, she said she didn't have time for sight-seeing; she had to finish the Camino by a certain date and fly home to go back to work. So some pilgrim lessons of the Camino were lost on her. To paraphrase St. Augustine, 'Don't search; stop and look.'

The corollary of this lesson was that I learned to trust my gut instinct. Not only did I from then on walk at my own pace, which was a consistent three miles per hour, but I did not adhere to the preset stopping points recommended by the guidebooks. I would decide to stop when I felt tired or when I just liked the look of a place.

❧ GUIDEBOOKS

A word on the guidebooks: Michelin has a useful version, and I saw another popular version by John Brierly. I used the 'Village to Village Guide to Hiking the Camino de Santiago' by Anna Dintaman and David Landis. This guidebook was very good and is updated yearly. The authors recommend stops every 20-25 kms or so, depending on the town, in order to break down the full Camino into 31 days of walking.

After that first day of over-achieving, I suffered and modified my thinking: from then on I stopped whenever I was tired, usually at about the 25-30 km (15-18 miles) point, depending on the town.

I also stopped as a general rule every two hours or so to have a coffee and a bite to eat, usually a slice of tortilla (Spanish omelets) or a ham and cheese sandwich on a baguette. Most importantly, this 15-20 minute stop rested my legs so that I could go on another two hours. I divided the day into two-hour segments, and including a lunch stop I could usually hit my daily objective after three stops, i.e. at around 15-18 miles.

As I started walking on the Camino I noticed many people used a staff. I remembered the staffs and the hiking poles used in the movie 'The Way' with Martin Sheen. I noticed different types: everything from the old – style gnarled wooden staff, taller than a person and measured to a four-count as you walked, to the high-tech telescoped titanium hiking poles that cost well over $100.

Of course I wanted badly to be a pilgrim, and it struck me that real pilgrims used the traditional staff, the 'bordon,' like that used by St. James himself. I checked out the metal hiking poles along with their prices, and found myself much more attracted to the staffs. They came in all shapes and sizes, and all types of wood. As pilgrims were leaving town all around me, I felt foolish shopping, so I quickly grabbed a bamboo staff. It cost only a few euros, but I liked it: it had an easy grip, was strong, and above all was lightweight.

I tried doing the four-count, holding the staff in my right hand and touching the ground well out in front of me and then counting four steps. I couldn't really do it, certainly not smoothly and not without thinking about it. I noticed others just held the staff much of the time, or used it more on the uphill than the downhill segments.

The walkers with the metal hiking poles were all over the map. A few people had the rhythm down, lightly touching with the left pole while pushing off with the right foot and vice versa. Easier said than done. Most users of hiking poles flailed about and didn't really get the full benefit from them. According to 'experts' – whoever they are – proper use of a staff or poles can take 15-20% of your weight from your legs, which would be very significant over the course of the Camino.

I saw people tie all sorts of things to the staffs, from decals to flowers. In a few cases people hung their towel or socks or even underwear to air dry while they walked.

More than anything, the users of hiking poles aggravated me with their noise. You could hear them coming up behind you, with the 'clack clack clack' of their poles. I tried not to be too judgmental. I felt that 'real pilgrims' don't use high tech hiking poles. Then again, 'real pilgrims' weren't so judgmental either.

I heard the click-click-click coming up behind me on a long stretch of the dusty Camino and wondered who my next friend would be. Without turning around, I wondered if it were someone I already knew or recognized from other towns or albergues. Once it was a Swedish man, well-built and using arm braces to propel along. Once we started talking, he told me he had had a hip replacement and was using the braces just to keep his balance and compensate a bit. Another time the clicking was a young woman on crutches, determined to finish the Camino even though her progress was slow and obviously painful.

This time it was a heavy-set man with a large pack and full beard who propelled himself next to me and instead of the typical 'Buen Camino!' said 'Bonjour!' I had run into plenty of French and Belgian pilgrims. I returned the 'Bonjour,' and then found out he was from a little town south of Montreal, Canada and his dream had always been to complete the Camino. He clicked along at such a pace that we didn't converse for very long before he pushed ahead and I resumed my steady rhythm.

I used my trusty staff, my sweaty grip gradually personalizing it, for a grand total of about four days before I left it in a truck stop.

◆ LODGINGS

Upon arrival in a town, I usually stayed in an albergue. These came in all sizes, and I learned to stay away from the large ones that hosted over 30 or so pilgrims, just based on the noise factor, which would make sleep difficult. After a couple of days of walking fifteen miles a day and sleeping poorly due to a snorer or other noise, one's body is exhausted. So every third night or so I would seek out an hostel or small hotel, usually costing about 25 euros, so I could get a private room and bathroom and get a good night's sleep.

The highlight of every day was arriving in an albergue or hotel, taking off one's boots, undressing, and showering. We called this process 'the pilgrim orgasm,' since it felt wonderful to wash the dirt off the road, get into different clothes and shoes, and then rest before going out to eat.

◆ FATHER JOY

Arriving in Grañon one afternoon after a long hot walk of over seven hours, I made my way to the San Juan Church, which I knew was a pilgrim albergue that, like many churches, operated on a donation basis. San Juan had been a pilgrim 'hospital' (in the sense of providing hospitality) for hundreds of years.

Outside the church in the rear garden I spotted a number of pilgrims lounging, massaging their feet and hanging their washed clothing on bushes. I was really looking forward to my 'Pilgrim Orgasm.' I then saw a figure dressed in a monk's cassock, barefoot, with long grey hair and a long unkempt grey beard, talking to pilgrims on a bench in the garden. I assumed he was a 'Santiago,' i.e. someone dressed as the Camino's patron saint, perhaps sponsored by the tourism bureau.

I checked into the albergue and was shown my mat, one of perhaps 40 in a large room where I would sleep that night. I finished my routine of showering and washing clothes, and then went across the plaza in front of the church to sit with fellow pilgrims and enjoy a glass of sangria.

I sat with a couple from San Diego, California, whom I had met in Santo Domingo de la Calzada a few hours earlier. We had a coffee together and they told me they were on the Camino to celebrate his 50th birthday. While on the Camino they enjoyed it so much they had decided to get married. They chose Cebreiro, a lovely town in Galicia, based on pictures of the church they had seen online. He ordered a tuxedo and she a wedding dress, which were being sent via FedEx to Spain.

I saw the two fellow countrymen sitting at the café in Grañon and joined them for sangría. We were joined by a young Irish woman who knew the American couple and had a good friendship with them. While we talked, I looked up and saw the figure of the barefoot monk approaching. He must have overheard the American-accented English and asked if he could sit down.

The 'monk' introduced himself as Father Joy of the Joyfulness Church of St. Christ.

'Saint Christ?' I asked.

'Yes, I consider him a saint, and much more. I deal with him directly. I call him Mister.'

'Mister Jesus or Mister Christ?' I asked. He did not answer.

In response to other questions, Father Joy said he was from Santa Cruz, California. When I asked if the Joyfulness Church of St. Christ was a religion, 'No,' he said. 'I don't need an interlocutor. I deal with Christ directly. He speaks to me.'

'So how did you come up with this idea for the Joyfulness Church?' I asked.

' In prison,' he responded.

I was eager to find out what Father Joy had been in prison for, but did not want to embarrass him. My chance came when I mentioned I planned to complete the Camino in the autumn with my daughter.

'I have a daughter,' he said. 'She lives with my parents, which is a good thing.'

'Oh, that's too bad she can't live with you,' I said.

'No, no,' he said. 'I'm all fucked up. I used to beat her Mom regularly, and one night I beat her to within an inch of her life, so I was sent to prison to get right.'

Father Joy said he had a benefactor who had donated a round trip airfare to Spain, and he made spending money by asking people for a one-euro donation every time he posed for a picture. He said he only needed one day's expenses at a time, so he asked for donations until he had about 25 euros, which would get him through the day. He said it took him very little time per day to collect the 25 euros.

He said he intended to complete the Camino. Noting that he was barefoot, I asked how far he went every day. 'About six kilometers,' he said, so a little more than three and a half miles.

'At that rate it might take you a year or more to complete the Camino,' I ventured. He said the time factor was not relevant to him. I thought back to my tourist stamp I received upon arrival at Madrid's Barajas Airport, which was good for three months. I wonder if Father Joy will be deported.

At the San Juan Church the priest held a Pilgrim Mass, which I attended. I saw that Father Joy was sitting a few pews in front of me.

When it came time for communion, I wondered what would happen. After all, I thought, to impersonate a priest is blasphemy. Would the priest offer Father Joy the wafer?

We all stood up in the aisle to get communion. Father Joy

then dramatically flipped up his cowl, which was a little too pointed for a monk's cassock, reminding me more of the KKK than of a monk. He approached the priest, lifting his clasped hands from a prayer-like position above his head into more of a Namaste position.

The priest gave him the wafer. As Father Joy received it he lifted up his left arm, bent at the elbow, and kept it raised for the next five minutes or so as he walked around the congregation before returning to his seat.

After Mass, the priest asked if anyone were interested in viewing some of his artifacts, including some saints' relics. I went into the enclosure to see the artifacts, and saw Father Joy prostrate on the floor, in sort of a child's pose, in front of the relics. He remained there for several minutes.

I asked the priest if he knew which saints these were, and he said no.

THE IRISHMAN

A small wiry old man with long grey hair and a beard walked into the albergue. In short order he stripped down to his shorts, did his laundry and went into the reception area to ask for beer.

He had multiple tattoos on his arms and legs. He sat down at a table with some German pilgrims and I overheard him say he had been in the Navy. He had a strong Irish accent.

He said he was doing two weeks of the Camino and then heading back to Belfast.

He heard another gentleman speaking English and introduced himself.

'Are you English?' he asked the gentleman.

'Yes. From Cambridge, actually,' he drawled in his best Oxbridge accent.

'Well I'm Irish,' he said, as if his accent hadn't already given him away.

'My wife was English,' he added.

'Oh, so she's no longer English?' the Cambridge man asked, snickering and thinking he was clever.

'I don't know,' said the Irishman. 'She's no longer my wife. I suppose she's still English.' And he walked away.

I spoke to the 'Englishman' later on that evening, and once you got past the carefully cultivated British accent he said he was actually from New Zealand but had been living in Cambridge, England for the past few years.

❖ INTUITION

At the albergues the pilgrims would typically first talk about injuries and then about how the albergues at the next stopping point in the guidebook were filling up. Many would then call ahead to reserve a place. As a result their day seemed to me more of a chore than an experience. I was unwilling to attach this level of organization to the Camino; to me it seemed to defeat the purpose.

Some pilgrims had printouts of all the albergues along the Camino, with evaluations on each – the best place to stay in each town, how much it cost, and what amenities it had, i.e. Wi-Fi, laundry, and total number of bunk beds. This struck me as way too organized.

While pilgrims gossiped about albergues filling up, in my experience it only happened once that I arrived in a town and had to inquire at three albergues before finding one that had a free bunk. I trusted my gut instinct, and over time that became a good lesson learned: there is nothing to fear, no reason to become anxious about albergues filling up. What is the worst-case scenario? If all the albergues were full (and some towns only had one or two), then I would try hostels, a casa rural (a room at someone's home), or a hotel. Intuition guided me to albergues. I would stop at one, take a look inside, invariably see someone I recognized, and decide either to keep moving or stop and take off my pack.

I decided the worst-case scenario would be sleeping in a field, using my backpack rain cover and windbreaker as a ground cloth. I was never worried about safety or crime; I would be perfectly safe sleeping in a field overnight. Once I realized that, then trusting my gut instinct became easier. I know that even until a few months ago I would have planned out a trip, sought reservations, and tried as much as possible to rule out variables.

I also liked to stop along the way, not just to take photos or have a coffee. Spain has over 4,000 castles and at least as many churches. Along the Camino many of these are in ruins, but I used my instincts to tell me when to stop and enter a church. Many were no more than small rural chapels, but some were remarkably beautiful. I recall one very old stone church near Santiago, with two versions of St. James represented in the same retablo. The uppermost one was St. James the 'Matamoros', and the larger one in the center was St James as a pilgrim, complete with a cassock, staff, and scallop shell.

I found that many pilgrims would walk right through a town and keep going, perhaps adhering to some schedule. I didn't, and I decided I couldn't have a schedule other than to make Santiago by the 8th of October at the latest, so that I could catch a train to Madrid and my flight back home the next day. I had general parameters but not a daily schedule. So I stopped in churches, took pictures in graveyards, and generally followed my gut.

My mental GPS and intuition worked well, especially during the first half of the Camino. Things began to get more complicated starting at Leon. I intended to start the second half of my Camino there, and the first night planned to stay at the Convent of the Benedictine Nuns, where one of my sons had stayed ten years earlier. It was a beautiful place on a small stone square in central Leon, but my daughter and I arrived on a weekend, and it was full. We then proceeded to call or visit at least half a dozen other places, all full. So much for my intuition.

At every stage of the Camino more people are joining. I finally found a small hotel on the outskirts of Leon, which would not have been my first choice, but worked out fine. Relying on my cellphone instead of my instincts was a bit jarring, however.

The next few stages were fine, and my daughter and I relied on our intuition to decide where to stay. My guidebook had a list of albergues and hotels with telephone numbers, but I had no idea which one was better than another. I knew from experience that there could be quite a difference between 9-euro albergues. Some were old and charming, others modern or beautifully restored, and some were just mildewy and dirty. I could have looked up each one online to search for comments, but that seemed to me to violate the Code of the True Pilgrim.

I wasn't sure what that was, but I somehow tried to maintain allegiance to it, minimizing my dependence on technology and going with my gut.

❧ THE MODERN QUIXOTE

At the San Juan Church in Grañon we not only slept all in one room on mats, but we also helped make dinner, clean up, and had a nice sesión of evening reflection after the Mass.

For dinner the two hospitalers, Gilda, a 35 year-old Italian woman and Ingrid, a 60 year-old German woman, had bought food with the money donated by pilgrims who stayed at the church the evening prior. Meals were basic, but in this case we had a salad, vegetable soup, and a local stew known as 'papas a la riojana,' or La Rioja – style potatoes. Basically it is potatoes with vegetables and bits of meat cooked in wine. When Ingrid started directing us how to slice potatoes and prepare the dish, a Spanish pilgrim interrupted and said 'That dish you are trying to make is 'papas a la riojana.' He knew how to prepare it and what proportions to apply of the wine and other ingredients. In the end the meal was hearty and filling – and healthy.

As it happened, I was next to the Spaniard at the long dining table seating perhaps 25 people. We struck up a conversation based on the dish he had choreographed, and I discovered he was from Galicia, specifically the coastal area of Lugo, north of Santiago de Compostela. Juan and I hit it off.

The next day I was out early, before first light, based on the Brazilian snorer's denial of sleep. Within the first couple of hours of my walk, Juan fell in next to me, and we talked all the way to our next stop.

In the end we slept in the same albergues, shared rooms in a couple of hostels, and got to know each other. Juan is a 35 year-old naval engineer, a proud 'gallego' (Galician) who knew Spanish cuisine and Spanish history.

We stopped for a coffee in the village of Ages at a tiny old stone inn with the name 'El Alquemista' (The Alchemist). The woman who attended recognized Juan's gallego accent and she too was Galician, so the two were like long-lost friends. As only Gallegos do, they discussed for twenty minutes the finer points of preparing fresh octopus.

'You have to have a large pot with lots of water, and bring

it to a boil before placing the octopus inside. Also, if when grabbing the octopus his tentacles wrap around your hand, then throw him away. The octopi should all be of the same size, say T4, since having small and large ones in the same pot will result in some being overcooked and others being rubbery. The octopus should be cooked no more than 20 minutes, and when cooled, should be cut with scissors.

The woman introduced herself as Maria Amapola (poppy, like the flower), an unusual but pretty name. She asked if I had seen the bright red poppies along the Camino.

'Of course,' I answered.

'They add color and happiness to the dull fields, and they grow in places where nothing else can grow, alongside roads, in ditches." She was exactly right, and from then on I thought of her description whenever I saw poppies. I also thought of her name as a metaphor for the Camino, since one found beauty and love in the most basic things.

Her home, an old inn, had a large entrance below for animals, and the people originally lived above them, benefitting from the animals' rising body heat. She showed me the old hole in the floor from the upper floor to the lower, explaining that that is where people would defecate, their excrement serving as fertilizer along with the animal excrement.

Maria Amapola loved talking about food. She said the best cure for a cold is 'sopa de caballo cansado' (tired horse soup), which is basically day-old bread soaked in warm wine. She said you give it to a child and it makes the child sweat, which gets rid of the fever, she said. I suspect the sleep, induced by the wine, is what would improve the child's health, not the wine itself.

She told me I would enjoy the local restaurants once I reached Galicia on the Camino because that region, along with the Basque Country, had the best food. She said I should eat plenty of octopus, cod ('bacalao'), grilled meats, suckling pig, and 'lechazo,' baby lamb. Asked the difference between a suckling lamb and a 'lechazo,' she said 'tits' ('tetas'). The suckling is still breast-feeding, while the lechazo has been weaned but is still a lamb.

She said Burgos had plenty of good 'lechazo' and it was a regional specialty. She recommended that when I arrive in Burgos Juan and I should find a place called La Maneli, since her friend ran the place, and to give her regards. We eventually did, and thoroughly enjoyed a plate full of roast lamb, a culinary feast compared to the basic meals we had been eating along the Camino.

Maria Amapola enjoyed our discussion so much that she yelled inside to have her husband put on some gaita music, which is based on bagpipes and is typically Galician. Juan of course beamed with pride, and I racked my brain wondering if the pagan Celts had brought the pipes to Galicia eons ago. Bagpipes in Spain?

Back on the road, Juan said his objective in doing the Camino was to soak up as much as he could about his native country, Spain. He said he had traveled widely around Europe and had been to Latin America and briefly to the U.S., but after much travel he realized that Spain had so much history and culture that he could spend years digesting it.

Juan worked as a naval engineer and had strong interests in robotics and artificial intelligence. He had made some investments that panned out, and so he returned to work on engineering assignments when he was tired of traveling. Asked when he would return to work, he liked to say 'When my money runs out.'

Juan researched historic towns and cities in Spain from the Roman times and other eras, and then downloaded an optimization program he found online, from a Stanford University professor, and organized the most efficient route. He spent three months traveling around southern and western Spain, taking in the old Roman cities of Caceres and Merida, where the emperors Hadrian and Trajan were from. He had been to every nook and cranny of the Iberian Peninsula. He started the Camino from St. Po on the French border, which is a week longer than the more common starting point of St. Jean Pied de Port.

At the same time he decided to focus on his nation's history and culture, Juan sold his possessions and bought books. He told me he read in the library of his town for an average of four hours every morning. He read philosophy and history, and went wherever the subject took him. He would quote Diogenes or St. Augustine as we walked, or the Spanish writers and poets such as Antonio Machado, Miguel de Unamuno or Federico Garcia Lorca.

Juan, in true pilgrim spirit, had no timetable. Unfortunately he developed an inflamed tendon in his shin, and although we sought out all sorts of remedies from creams, balms, to heavy ibuprofen doses, the swelling and pain was so bad that he had to go to the clinic in Leon. The doctors took one look at his leg and said he just needed rest for at least a few days, total repose. They also gave him stronger anti-inflammatory medicine. I left him there in Leon, and since then I have received Whats App messages from him telling me he is back on the Camino and has reached his native Galicia. As he likes to say, he is going home, so it doesn't matter where he goes or when he gets there.

Along the Meseta from Burgos to Leon, a relatively flat dull portion of the Camino, we talked about the group of Crusaders known as the Knights Templars, who in between Crusades spent their time in Spain protecting the pilgrims. The Knights Hospitalers did this as well. He told me how the French King, deeply in debt to the Templars, had their head, Jacques de Molay, arrested and tortured into making a false confession (which de Molay recanted). The King then had de Molay burned at the stake. Before the fire was lit, de Molay famously put a curse on France. In addition, he was burned on a Friday the 13th, which is believed to be the origin of our modern tradition that this day is bad luck.

We talked of El Cid, of the Spanish-born Roman emperors, and of how the road we were on was the old Via Acquia, which the Romans built. The Roman 7th Legion was based in Leon, and protected the gold mined in Galicia and its shipment to Rome. Romans built many of the bridges, and planted wine grapes, wheat, and other staples to feed their legion.

Juan mentioned that at a bridge on the Orbio River in Castile, just outside Leon, a knight named Don Suero de Quiñones challenged any man who wanted to cross the bridge to a joust. His challenge was based on a promise from his lover, who said that if he 'broke 300 lances' then she would accede to his love. Accordingly, Don Suero took ten of his men, all knights, and they encamped at the bridge to challenge every knight to a joust. It is said that after defeating 166 challengers Don Suero and his men were injured to the point where they gave up. It is not known whether his lover gave in at that point or not, but his exploits did gain the atention of Miguel de Cervantes, who used Don Suero as a prototype of his errant knight Don Quixote.

'And Don Quixote still lives!' I said.

'What do you mean?,' asked Juan.

'You, Juan are the modern Quixote. You must press on, insist on having your adventures, until – like the Quixote – someone tells you there is another reality and you need to snap out of it.'

"We both know there is another reality. But we prefer this one.'

❧ LANDSCAPE

The Camino begins 'at your door,' people like to say, since 'all roads lead to Santiago.' In fact there are many Caminos in Spain, the so-called 'Frances' being the traditional route and by far the most traveled. There is a 'Camino del Norte' which extends from the Pyrenees to Santiago along the Basque coast-line. It is longer and more difficult terrain than the Frances. The 'Camino Ingles' ('The English Way') goes from Ferrol in Galicia straight south to Santiago, a walk of about 5-7 days. It is named the 'English Camino' because Celts and Irish used to travel to the Galician coast in longboats from the earliest days and then proceed inland to 'compostela' – the field of stars – where they held pagan rituals way before Romans ever came to Iberia.

There are many others: the 'Camino de la Plata', which goes from Sevilla to Santiago traversing western Spain – Extremad-ura – and even a 'Camino del Cid,' which goes from El Cid's native Burgos southeast, stopping at his main battle victory spots, all the way to Alicante and Valencia.

In St. Po and St. Jean Pied de Port in the French Pyrenees, the Camino crosses into Spain's Basque Region, which has a culture all its own and a language whose origin is ancient and unknown. The Basque Country is fiercely proud of its culture and its contributions to Spanish culture, from the navigator Sebastian Elcano to Jesuit founder Ignacio de Loyola. A Basque is a Basque first, not a Spaniard. In the past generation the Basques have successfully negotiated a degree of autonomy, and in return for their acceptance of a central government in Madrid they have benefitted immensely from Spanish infrastructure investment.

The Basque Region arguably has the best cuisine in Spain, and one of the best in the world, at least when judged by Michelin stars. Seven of the eight 3-Star Michelin restaurants in Spain are in the Basque Region, and the eighth, in Madrid, is a Basque restaurant. Their fresh seafood is simple and spectacular.

The Camino Frances, the most traditional of the pilgrimage routes, winds through mountainous terrain much of the first week and then descends to the foothills in La Rioja, the main wine-growing region of Spain. Logroño, the capital of the region, has been growing grapes since the Romans planted them a thousand years ago. Logroño is also famous for having perhaps the best quality pintxos in Spain. Pintxos are high-end tapas, a little more elaborate and purchased separately, whereas in many parts of Spain a tapa is included with a glass of beer or wine.

From La Rioja the Camino flattens out into Castille and Leon, going through the Ribera del Duero región (again a superb wine producer), and an agricultural región. The cured meats, especially morcilla (blood sausage) are very good in this región. I had varied types of morcilla in Burgos, each one with a different combination of spices. In this agricultural region, the cheeses were also fresh and strong, especially the sheep's cheese (mainly manchego).

Castilla and Leon are generally flat and agricultural, and are generally considered the most boring part of the journey. In the summer months, it is also very hot, reaching over ninety degrees farenheit. I found this portion to be sometimes endless, but the solitude and the great stretches of distance between towns left one alone with his own thoughts, so as a result I found this segment introspective, and probably closer to the pilgrim experience of the Middle Ages.

✦ THE IRON CROSS

The route from the town of Najera went steeply uphill and into the woods. Old records of the Camino recorded that this area was dangerous for its brigands and outlaws who robbed passersby. It was a long uphill climb, followed by a second and then a third hill. Between the hills I passed through Atapuerca, a small archeological dig that contains some of the oldest remnants of man, dating back one million years.

At the top of the third hill there was a circle of stones on the right side of the Camino. I wondered if the circle were part of some ancient pagan ritual, or if they were a visual reference for pilots. There was a sign mentioning a military base nearby, so it occurred to me the circle could even be for target practice.

At the top of the last hill you can see Burgos and the spires of its cathedral in the distance. Since I had already walked about 15 miles that day, I decided to stop in the next small town overnight, which would leave me with an easy six or seven mile walk into Burgos the next morning.

On that same hill was a large iron cross overlooking the valley of Burgos. The base of the cross was a mound of countless stones and mementos, prayers left by pilgrims over many years.

My parents lived in Spain for many years, and my mother died in Spain. While they have both long since passed away, I know they loved Spain and would have stayed the rest of their lives. Accordingly I carried with me to Spain my father's Korean War dog tags with a cross on the chain, and when I reached the famous iron cross of the Camino I buried one of his dog tags among the prayer stones, and said a prayer for my parents. I noticed that there were hundreds, if not thousands of other stones, mementos, and objects on which people had written prayers or names of loved ones around the world.

◆ RIOPICO

From the cross I walked down the steep hill in an S-shaped pattern so as to reduce the pressure on the knees and ankles. The Camino wound steeply to Villalva and then to Urdeñuela de Riopico, my destination for the evening.

I checked into the very small albergue. I was very tired after climbing the three hills, and was really looking forward to my pilgrim routine, i.e. shower, change, eat and rest. The proprietor was gruff and curt, and insisted on showing me the rates and eating options by flipping through I-Pad screens. I had to wait patiently as he showed me each overnight rate with and without dinner options, on successive I-Pad screens.

My pilgrim credential stamped, the proprietor yelled at his assistant to get the rooms ready. When the assistant left the room he said, 'That guy is so stupid. We have anti-lice covers on the beds and once a week we spray the zippers of the sheets with the strongest bug spray on the market. It's a pretty simple process: you first close the windows and spray, and then you exit the room, closing the door as you leave. This idiot,' he said gesticulating towards the assistant 'sprays and then opens the window complaining he's dizzy and has a headache. Leave the room after you spray, you moron!' he laughed.

After completing the Pilgrim Orgasm I went back into the reception where I again found the manager, this time fuming about his countrymen. When I commented that I rarely encountered Spaniards on the Camino, he said they constituted perhaps 20% of the total, adding that he counted Basques and Catalans as Spaniards even though they didn't. He raised an eyebrow as he said it, adding in a hushed tone – 'It's all about money. They threaten independence so the central government will send them more money. Like blackmail. These provinces are demanding a ransom!' he said.

The owner's Venezuelan wife came into the reception area and the two sat down to eat. I stayed with them, talking and mainly listening as the owner obviously had a lot to say.

'The Spaniards are the worst. They call and reserve and then never call back to cancel, so I end up eating the cost of the room. That's a lack of respect!,' he said. Most other nationalities, he said, have the courtesy to cancel if they can't honor a reservation.

Between phrases he swore in phrases only the Spanish use, and with great effect. Each sentence was punctuated by 'joder!' ('Fuck!') or 'Me cago en Dios!' ('I shit on God!', which flows in Spanish but really jars in English.)

'Have I told you how stupid my assistant is?,' he asked.

'Yes,' I responded, mentioning the bug spray incident.

'That's nothing. Another day he was mowing the grass and he stopped suddenly, grabbing his head in pain. It turned out he had been stung by a bee on the head. I found the swelling and put a bandage on it.

Five minutes later he's mowing again, then stops and runs back over to me while grabbing his head. Again I find he has been stung, I find the spot and put a bandage on it. He returns to the lawn mower and this time I watch him. It turns out he was mowing under a tree and each time he pushed forward he hit his head against a beehive, which caused the bees to attack. I told him to forget about mowing under the tree. He never would have figured it out.'

◆ FARMACIAS

Since I developed blisters the first day after going too far in the heat, I hobbled like many other pilgrims for the entire first week. At one stop an Italian showed me the proper way to lance, drain, and disinfect a blister to enable continued walking. He graciously used his own supplies on me, so I needed to find a pharmacy to buy my own scissors, tape, and disinfectant.

Spain's 'farmacias' are wonderful. Along the Camino, pilgrims who are greatly in need of ointments, bandages, and other basics, prize the farmacias. The problem is that farmacias tend to be only in the larger towns, so one has to keep walking sometimes a day or two before finding one. As a result, a common topic of conversation among pilgrims was the mention that 'in the next town there is a farmacia.' Nodding of heads, smiles.

And going into one as a pilgrim was a delight. The pharmacists were always considerate and understanding, and at this point, after a millennium of pilgrims walking the Camino, they are the world's experts on blisters and general foot/leg pain issues. In addition, the pharmacists and their assistants are used to dealing with this motley international clientele.

I had a fellow pilgrim instruct me in the lore of blisters and their care, so that once I reached a farmacia I knew what to buy: Betadine, the antiseptic, nail scissors for cutting open and draining the blister, and Cupeed, a padded adhesive that is placed on top of the blister and left there for days until it falls off. I also procured adhesive tape that I used liberally on my heels and any hot spot that might develop into a blister.

Perhaps best of all, the farmacias in Spain had Ibuprofen in 600 mg tablets. In the U.S. the standard dose is 200 mg tablets, and doctors recommend not more than 600mg a day. I only used 'vitamin I,' as it is called, when needed, which was every day. When I stopped walking in the afternoon I would take one tablet, and when I went to sleep I would take two more, totaling the 600mg daily limit.

The U.S. packaging on Ibuprofen warns that extended of excessive use of Ibuprofen could cause 'cardiovascular thrombotic events,' heart attacks, and even gastrointestinal bleeding, including perforating the stomach.

Fortunately I was fine at 600mg a day. My fellow pilgrim Juan was suffering from an ankle injury that morphed into swelling on the ligament in front of the ankle. He was in serious pain as we approached Burgos, and he treated it with an anti-inflammatory cream and about 1800mg/day of Spanish Ibuprofen as we crossed the Meseta to Leon. As we reached Leon his lower leg was swollen and he told me 'no doy otro paso' ('I can't take another step'). He went to a clinic and was given a prescription for a stronger pain killer and anti-inflammatory, and told to rest for at least three days. Unlike most pilgrims who are given medical advice to rest, Juan followed the advice and as a result was able to continue and complete the Camino.

◆ INTENTIONS

My blisters were bothering me one day, so I cut it short and stopped for the night at an albergue in the little town of Hornillo del Camino.

After completing my ritual of bathing, washing clothes, and eating, I walked to the tiny town square (grandly called the 'Plaza Mayor') and sat down with a glass of red wine.

The tiny square has a fountain in the shape of an obelisk with a rooster on top. Supposedly, the rooster commemorates the theft by occupying French troops of every chicken in the city. The French soldiers hid the chickens in their drums and denied the theft until a chicken escaped and made a racket.

I greeted pilgrim friends passing by, and was joined by

a traveling group from Belgium, as happens every day along the Camino.

Of the three travelers, one stuck out: a striking blonde woman, her head thrown back in laughter. Her hair was long but gathered on top of her head, and she had a natural smile showing perfect teeth. Her two male companions focused conversation towards her; she was the main attraction. Her name was Madeleine.

Her companion was a fresh-faced boyish man of about 30, a financial planner in Brussels. He was easily five or more years younger than the woman.

The third companion was a Hungarian from Slovakia. He had a rugged complexion, dark eyes and a three-day growth of beard and his eyes showed that he had already been drinking.

When the banker (Christophe) went to the bar to buy more wine, his traveling companion explained that she was not with him but had met him on the Camino. She said she was married but that her husband was back in Belgium.

Asked about her reason for undertaking the Camino, she looked down, shook her head and said she had some problems and wanted to get away.

'It's also a big commitment in terms of training, getting the right gear, and devoting enough time to the journey,' I offered.

'Not in my case. I decided to come on the Camino three days before getting on the train to Spain. I'm just getting away I guess,' she said, still looking at the ground.

I let her comment hang in the air in silence until the banker returned with a round of drinks. He brought orujo, the very strong locally-made liquor made from boiling and condensing wine.

'Let's celebrate,' he said.

'I don't think so. I don't drink hard liquor,' I said.

Two days later I saw Madeleine on a park bench in the town of Fromista. She was with another man, talking and eating. She did not see me, and thinking of her earlier personal comments I walked on, not wanting to cause any embarrassment.

◆ BURGOS

The Burgos Cathedral was spectacular. It contains some of the most impressive altars in Spain, and is the burial place of Rodrigo Diaz de Vivar, known as El Cid. Vivar is a small town not far away, near Zamora. El Cid was a hero in battle against the Moors, driving them south and east toward Valencia, where he was wounded and died.

The Burgos Cathedral is especially beautiful in the early morning light. I left the city through the impressive stone walls that surround it, then through parks and past the university.

◆ MURDER IN THE CATHEDRAL

At Grañon about 30 of us pilgrims slept on the floor of the church, on mats. We shared all cooking and washing chores, and the priest celebrated a pilgrim Mass for us. We had a 'time for reflection' after dinner when people volunteered to speak up and articulate their feelings. Some thoughts were lofty and philosophical, others very personal. It struck me how pilgrims feel an implicit trust. Everyone is quite open about their feelings, explaining why they are on a pilgrimage. And there is no theft; in fact I never even heard tell of anyone's belongings going missing.

As we lay down on our mats I noticed mine was right next to a very large Brazilian man. I had spoken with him a couple of times as we passed along the route, and I noticed he called home and spoke to his wife in Brazil every night. I had passed him at least three times over the course of a week or so, so I finally figured out that he started walking earlier and finished later than most of the rest of us.

But the Brazilian was a powerful snorer. Not just snoring but occasional snorting and guttural sounds emitted from him. There was no way I could sleep there. I picked up my mat and sleeping sack and went upstairs to sleep on the kitchen floor.

Snoring is an issue at albergues. If you encounter a really strong one, then nobody can sleep more than a few winks, and everyone is exhausted and knows they have another 25 kms to go the next day.

In one albergue a young German man – who by the way insisted on sleeping in his bikini briefs – snored in a manner that sounded like two wild boars fighting. It was a relatively tight pack of bunk beds, so there was no escaping.

The second problem with albergues was that pilgrims,

especially if there is a heavy snorer in their midst, get up at four or five o'clock in the morning to get a head start on the day's walking.

So if you are sleeping on the kitchen floor, as I was in Grañon, or with the bikini-clad German, you can't sleep in because all around you people are getting up, rooting in their backpacks, and going back and forth to the bathroom.

As she walked out the door of one albergue around 5:30am, I heard one woman say ' I just can't take it anymore!,' as she slammed the door to the sleeping area.

Over coffee at a rest stop, four or us who had been at the bunk-bed albergue with the German were discussing how poorly we had slept and how tired we were. One demure Canadian woman stated 'Well, there's no getting around it. We need our sleep!' Others agreed, nodding and then laughing about the snorers. The demure Canadian woman then said 'We should kill them.'

Everyone fell silent. After all this sort of statement was not exactly in the pilgrim spirit.

The Canadian woman added 'Nobody would ever know. I mean, it's an albergue. There's at least fifty people in there, all of whom have a motive.'

We all laughed. 'Right! 'Murder in the Albergue.' Unsolved mystery.' 'And nobody will suspect us pious pilgrims.'

◆ PILGRIM ETIQUETTE?

Not all cultures are equal when it comes to the nature of shame. I mentioned the bikini-clad German snorer. When some central European women raised their arms you could see the voluminous armpit hair. Others paraded about in their panties and a t-shirt, completely oblivious to those of us who were careful to look away.

Further on the cultural differences, there is a sort of code of behavior when walking the Camino. If one needed to pass gas, for example, you might at least look around to see if there was another pilgrim just behind you. A Spaniard I spoke to was miffed that some otherwise polite and attractive girls walking in front of him just let loose some farts that almost blew him over. 'Is there no pilgrim etiquette?,' he asked.

◆ ANGEL

About an hour's walk west from Hontanas I saw ruins and an archway over the Camino. This was San Anton, named for Saint Anthony. There is an ancient pilgrims hospital there, which today houses the albergue. St. Anthony's distinctive Tau Cross is on the arches. This site once held relics from St. Anthony, the Third Century monk from Egypt.

Across the road from the ruins is a bar. I was not going to stop since I had only walked one hour from Hontanas, but the distinctive American music of Ella Fitzgerald lured me inside like a Pied Piper.

The man swaying to the music with his eyes closed, standing behind a ramshackle bamboo bar, was Angel, the burly proprietor who greeted me effusively. He offered wine in a wineskin (bota) although it was only about 9 am. I declined and asked for coffee.

Angel showed off his technique with the bota, squirting the wine while extending his arm fully. He then upped the ante by aiming the wine next to his nose, allowing it to run down the outside of his nostril and into his mouth.

'Do you believe this Korean kid came here this morning asking for Cachimbol?,' he asked.

'Where did he ever hear about Cachimbol?' The drink he was referring to is a mix of cheap red wine and Coca-cola. Students in Spain sometimes order it since it is a cheap, quick way to get drunk.

Angel next turned his attention to a Romanian woman, a pilgrim. 'You are so beautiful. You must be a model,' he beamed.

The woman calmly said no, adding that she was far too old to be a model.

'It is experience that gives a woman maturity and makes her really attractive,' Angel tried.

The woman ignored him. He turned back to me, and I asked if he were going to keep trying out different lines with the woman, like putting coins into a slot machine until he hit the jackpot. Flashing his rakish smile, he responded 'God knows how many times I've had my heart broken.'

Angel asked where I was from and I asked him about his past. He had been in finance in Madrid, and quit after doing the Camino for the first time. He decided to set up a small business in San Anton but it failed, as did his next two ventures. His current place, the bamboo bar, was not going well financially but, he said, his 'income' was psychic: he got to meet pilgrims all day long.

He explained that 'Just as we are talking now and enjoying each other's company, we are participating in the spirit of the Camino as true pilgrims. We don't care about each other's name, our past, and our jobs in the real world.

'Let me give you an example,' he said. You are from Washington D.C. What is the biggest avenue in that city?'

'Constitution Avenue,' I answered.

'OK, you return to your city, walk down Constitution Avenue, and you say hello to everyone, wave hi, and help everyone you can. What will happen? You will be committed to an insane asylum in 15 minutes!'

We laughed together, but I understood his point. At this bend in the road in San Anton, in the bamboo bar with Ella Fitzgerald reminding me of my 'other world' back home, Angel was articulating the attraction of the Camino.

◆ PACO

I walked most of the way between Castrojeriz and Itero de la Vega with Paco, a 50-ish Spaniard from Galicia. In fact, he lives in a suburb of Santiago de Compostela, so we laughed that he was really just walking home.

Being from Santiago, Paco was of course very familiar with the Camino, and had done various short portions of it but never the entire thing.

He said he swore when his son was born that he would walk the Camino in thanks. His son is now sixteen years old. What drove Paco to finally undertake the journey was a surgical procedure he had last year to remove a small tumor in his brain. He swore while in the hospital that if he recovered he owed God a Camino.

I got to know Paco well, and we shared meals and walked together on and off for the next week.

◆ REST

At the end of my first week as I reached Burgos I decided to treat myself to a hotel room.

When checking into the hotel I was shocked when I heard the price of 35 euros. What? I had been paying five euros a night, sometimes ten, for albergues. So 35 seemed like a lot of money, until I thought what a cheap motel would cost along a roadside in the rural U.S.

I was sore and had my blisters, but they were healing and I was already 'through the pain' by the time I arrived in Burgos. I deliberately stayed about ten kms short of the city so that I could walk into it early in the morning and spend more time there seeing the sights, particularly the cathedral. The approach to Burgos is one of the least attractive parts of the Camino, basically an industrial park. Some of the guidebooks recommend taking a bus these last ten kms to avoid the congested roads and factories, but that was never really a consideration for me. I insisted on walking.

I decided the best thing I could do for my body was 24 hours of rest. One of my fellow pilgrims – an expert on physical maladies of all kinds, like so many pilgrims seemed to be – said my body was probably in shock after a week of the daily grind of walking. It didn't matter how you trained prior to coming to Spain, nobody could replicate 6-7 hours of walking per day over that length of time.

So the next morning I covered the 10 kms quickly and arrived well before noon, and was able to check in to a small hotel close to the cathedral. The best part of having one's own hotel room, aside from not having to share it with fifty of my closest snoring buddies, was the sense of space. I was used to a tiny space and considered myself lucky when there was a chair next to my bunk. I also thoroughly enjoyed the luxury of privacy. I took everything out of my backpack and spread them out on the bed. I washed some things in the bathroom (my own bathroom!), showered and then napped for hours.

I got dressed and visited the cathedral, which is one of Europe's great gothic churches, and took the audio tour. I ran into other pilgrims I knew, and waved but did not want to engage.

I met up with Juan for a glass of wine, and he was eager to show me the Municipal Albergue. Since most albergues we knew were fairly modest affairs, I was pleasantly surprised and impressed when he took me into this fairly new albergue, with three floors of bunk bed-filled rooms and even an elevator. I almost – almost – wanted to stay there instead of my private hotel room.

After dinner I went back to my room at an early hour – pilgrim hours are early by definition and by necessity, and totally at variance with traditional Spanish hours – and I was asleep by 9:30 pm. I decided I would get up whenever I awoke, and not push myself get up and out in the early morning, as I had for the previous two weeks. I woke up at 7am, later than usual, and actually felt a little guilty. I was thinking how the Municipal Albergue would likely be empty by now, everyone having packed up and left by 6:30. I packed up my things (which takes about 60 seconds), got dressed, and had a breakfast at the hotel, which was included in the price of the room. I then left, having rested almost 24 hours, and feeling creaky but good.

As I left the city I noticed the cathedral is especially beautiful in the early morning light. Now as I passed through the impressive medieval walls that surround the town, I knew I was heading into the Meseta, the flattest, hottest part of the Camino.

⬥ MESETA

My mind wandered, as it often did on the Camino, especially on the Meseta between Burgos and Leon. This is a flat, monotonous portion of the Camino, which some guidebooks recommend skipping since it does not tend to have the picturesque villages or historical monuments of interest. I disagree completely.

I found this central portion of the Camino peaceful and contemplative. In medieval times pilgrims often got lost in this area because it is relatively featureless and monotonous. At the same time, it is referred to as the 'mental' portion of the Camino. The first part through the Basque and Navarre countryside to Burgos is the 'physical' portion. And the last part, from Leon to Santiago over the mountains into Galicia, is the 'spiritual' part.

I had been told the Meseta was boring, and that nasty weather could hit at any time. There was no shade, and in May when I passed through it was hot. I was more alone on the Meseta than anywhere on the Camino, perhaps because there were fewer pilgrims walking, or perhaps it just felt that way because of the vast expanse of the countryside.

My experience was the opposite of what I had heard. I could see how someone would think it relatively boring in terms of sightseeing, but then again that wasn't why I was there.

The Roman 7th Legion built the road I was on, and planted the cultivated fields on each side. Red poppies lined the road as far as the eye could see. I could see giant wind generators on the far hills, their blades still in the heat.

I could walk for an hour or more in the 180-degree expanse of Spanish sky without seeing another pilgrim. The countryside had few man-made structures of any kind, but the rolling low hills were beautiful.

I learned more about myself on the Meseta than on any other part of the Camino, mainly because I was alone with my thoughts for extended periods. The solitude and the vulnerability to nature also made the experience spiritual.

There were no distractions. Time to confront your demons, go inside yourself and dream. Memories float to the surface, some of them welcome, others not. I found I could analyze things dispassionately out on the Meseta, stripped of all else, just the beating sun and thinking about putting one foot in front of the other for what seemed like an eternity. It was very peaceful, and I understood that what I considered anxieties or problems were relatively insignificant. Put in perspective, I understood I had either limited or no control over them. With that realization I felt a positive surge of energy, and I pressed on, smiling.

I loved the expanse of the Meseta, and felt close to nature. I was exposed. The sun beat down on me, and if it were going to rain, there was no shelter. In short, I felt more like a pilgrim on the Meseta than anywhere else on the Camino.

I learned something else on the Meseta: setting and making goals. Walking in that expanse, heading west along the Camino, one can see the mountains in the distance. You know you need to cross those mountains to get to Santiago, yet they seem impossibly far away. Within a week or so after Leon you look back and realize you have crossed the Meseta, a week's worth of walking. What seemed like forever is over.

From there you go up foothills, then hills, and then through the mountains at O Cebreiro, probably the steepest climb of the Camino. Standing in the mist in the lovely stone village of O Cebreiro you have a feeling of accomplishment.

You can go virtually any distance one day at a time, broken down into my routine of coffee and snack breaks every two hours or so. I now knew I can attain goals incrementally, breaking them into small pieces, one step at a time. This realization in turn gave me confidence.

To me the Meseta was indeed the 'mental' part of the Camino, and perhaps the 'spiritual' part as well. One pilgrim told me an Italian priest told him the Camino was divided into three sections, and when I said 'I know, physical, mental, and spiritual, right?' He said no. The first stage, from St. Jean to Burgos, represents life, with its highs and lows, its challenges. The second stage, the Meseta, represents death, since it feels transcendent and limitless. And the third stage, as you reach Santiago, represents the rebirth of a new you.

◆ DRONES?

I would guess about 10-20 percent of Pilgrims are Asian, divided pretty evenly between Koreans and Japanese. For some reason the pilgrimage does not interest the Chinese, or perhaps I just didn't meet any.

The Asians are easily recognizable from a distance. They are covered, head to toe, to minimize exposure to the sun. They tend to use wide-brim hats, long pants, long sleeves, and in some cases bandanas or masks covering the lower half of the face.

The Koreans and Japanese stayed in the albergues alongside everyone else, but they tended to buy and prepare their own food along the way.

One young Japanese man was constantly taking pictures, filming, and checking GPS coordinates. Over the course of a few days, I saw this was a consistent pattern of behavior. During one rest stop I asked him what he was filming or recording. Turns out he is a television producer in Japan, and he is taking lots of footage, including geo-coordinates, along the Camino. What's more, he has a small drone and was directing it above us, taking pictures and filming towns and the countryside.

◆ BLACK WIDOW

A Croatian woman told me the same day that she spent almost no time preparing for the Camino. She took unpaid leave from her job as an airline flight attendant and went to Nepal, hiked and then spent a month studying meditation through silence. Once she finished the month, she cast about for other ways to reach a state of peace within herself. She fastened on the Camino, borrowed a backpack and basic gear from friends and from her sister, and traveled to Biarritz, crossing the border by train and starting the Camino at St. Jean. She has unpaid leave for another month so she is wondering what else she can do in the remaining time to increase her understanding.

After walking in silence for awhile, she said ' You know, in my Nepalese meditation class they called me the spider, you know, the black one that kills.'

'You mean the black widow?' I asked.

'Exactly.'

I let that remark hang in the air a bit, then decided to change the subject and keep walking.

◆ THE CONQUISTADORS

I arrived in the town of Castrojeriz in the early afternoon. I decided to get a hotel room so I could avoid the noise and snoring of the albergue. I checked in, did my pilgrim routine of bathing and washing, and decided to get something to eat before resting.

I wondered if I would continue my pilgrim routine once I returned to 'civilization.' Would I only use two t-shirts, two pair of underwear and two pair of socks, and wash them by hand daily?

I found a small bar with outdoor seating, and although the day was hot there was a pleasant breeze outside under an awning. I ordered the two-course pilgrim meal for 10 euros, which seems to be the standard price in this area. The pilgrim meal consists of a first course, second course, dessert, wine and coffee.

A 60 year-old man wearing a weathered blue sweatshirt, khakis and sneakers with no socks or laces occupied the only other outside table. The sweatshirt said 'Soggy Dollar Bar, BVI.' Since I know that bar and it is a tiny place, I asked him about traveling to the BVI.

He responded that he loved his trip to the BVI over a year ago with his girlfriend.

I noticed he was drawing so I asked about that. He motioned me closer and I saw he was actually drawing with pen and painting with watercolors. He was painting the Santa Maria Church, a XII century Romanesque beauty.

He then showed me his sketchbook, which was full of churches and scenes from the Camino.

His name was Emilio. He was traveling in a 1960 model 'Willy' WWII era jeep, recording the Camino with a Go Pro camera and stopping at each major location and picking out a church or site. He said he always included a pilgrim in each picture since the Pilgrim is the focus of the Camino.

Emilio explained that he had a fake hip and was unable to walk the route. But he was always fascinated by it, and as a trained architect he is a gifted freehand drawer, so he is applying his talents to the Camino.

Emilio said he had four grown children but that his daughter was depressed and he felt she would benefit from the spirit of camaraderie and community on the Camino. So he was dedicating his sketchbook to her in hopes it would motivate her to undertake her own pilgrimage. He said she needs something to lift her spirits. 'The Camino is what she needs,' he said.

Pilgrims on the Camino were uniformly positive, helpful, and giving, and despite the obvious language barriers, nobody had any trouble communicating. Our concerns were shared: everyone was tired, everyone had sore or blistered feet, and everyone was called to undertake the pilgrimage. There was a clear 'pilgrim spirit' that permeated the group, and it is this that attracted pilgrims to return over and over again. It was as if the Holy Spirit flowed east to west along the Camino, all the way to Santiago.

♦ REV. WREN

I came across the small, simple grave marker of Reverend Philip Wren, alongside the Camino in a remote area. A sapling had been planted next to the marker. Upon my return to 'the real world' I looked up Reverend Wren and found out he was an Englishman, a Methodist Minister from Liverpool, who had passed away while undertaking the Camino. He apparently died in his sleep at an albergue in Logroño while on his tenth Camino.

◆ LEON

I reached Leon after a week walking the Meseta. This was to be my last stop on the first half of the Camino, so I booked a small hotel room as a treat to myself. I met up with friends that night, and early the next morning walked to the bus station and took the bus to Madrid to begin my voyage home.

In Leon I noticed pilgrims calling taxis to the bus and train stations because they were done: they were doing the Camino from St. Jean to Burgos (two weeks) or from Logroño to Burgos (one week). I had a number of pilgrims tell me they were doing one or two weeks this year and would complete the Camino over two or three years. Others had limited time off from work. Many of the Spaniards I encountered were using one week of their vacation to walk a portion of the Camino.

I don't know the percentages, but many pilgrims also drop out due to family emergencies or to physical problems – blisters and joint pain, most commonly, or inflammation like my friend Juan from Galicia. Later on, when I reached Santiago, I was told that only ten percent of pilgrims do the entire Camino at one time.

PART II:
LEON TO SANTIAGO

Two months later I was heading back with my daughter to finish the Camino, doing the Leon to Santiago portion. I was eager to return to the pilgrim life on the Camino. It had its hardships but one was surrounded by good, interesting people who cared for each other and who were serious about their intentions.

I had two months back home to distill my experiences before my daughter recuperated fully from her ligament damage and we scheduled our return to Spain. Fortunately, she is also fluent in Spanish. She was very deliberate in her preparations, and was worried about the physical toll it would take. I responded that since she is a runner and a yoga enthusiast, I was not worried about her body; only about the feet.

We met in New York and flew to Madrid to catch the bus to Leon.

On the plane on the way to Spain I thought back to the blisters, the heat, the snorers in the albergues. Tell me again: why am I doing this? And now I'm dragging my daughter with me.

Why would I go back to that lifestyle? Every morning for weeks I got up before sunrise, tiptoed to the bathroom trying not to make noise among the bunk beds, and packed up my belongings into my backpack. I slipped on my shorts and a jacket, went outside to put on my boots, and then tried to find the nearest yellow arrow marker to put me back on the Camino. I walked in the cold and dark, using my cellphone as a flashlight, looking for a place that served coffee.

I kept walking for six or seven hours, sometimes more, taking breaks every two hours or so, until I covered 15-20 miles and felt tired. I used my intuition to step into the right albergue, and then start my other routine: washing, bathing, and resting.

I would find a place for dinner, and be back in my sleeping bag by 9:30pm. I did this every day, bringing me closer to Santiago de Compostela.

I thought about how, as I go through this routine, all along the 500 miles of the Camino thousands of other pilgrims are going through the same routines as me, walking from France all the way across Spain, to a place where the bones of St. James supposedly lie. We are all doing this.

Everyone has their reason for being on the Camino, from simple tourism to amazing stories of love and devotion.

As I sat on the airplane reflecting, I realized I loved the feeling of the Camino, meeting people from all over the world, being alone with my thoughts, and pushing toward a goal that made sense to me.

I also very much looked forward to spending two weeks with my 25 year-old daughter. She is an impressive woman, and I was flattered and humbled she wanted to join me.

◆ GOODWILL

Virgilio is a 70 year-old Spaniard from Leon who travels back and forth on the Camino between Leon and Santiago. He looks like Kris Kringle and is dressed like a priest in a long black cassock with a flat black Pilgrim hat, his bordon, and a scallop shell tied around his neck.

Virgilio's bordon is unlike most others. He fastens flowers, at least one rose or carnation, with a rubber band to the top of the bordon. And he sings as he walks. His calling is to bring happiness to traveling pilgrims.

Virgilio told me that that morning he came across a young American girl sitting crying along the side of the Camino. She heard his singing as he approached, and lifted her head. He stopped in front of her, smiled and continued singing. Finally she stopped crying and broke out into a smile.

Virgilio told me this is what he tries to do every day: bring happiness to the pilgrims along the Camino. He likes to sing, and singing breaks down barriers and makes people happy, he said. He said his wife back in Leon gets a little upset with him because he has now accumulated a roomful of mementos from the Camino, and their small apartment is too crowded as it is. But, he said, I am on the Camino most of the time, so she can't get too upset with me.

◈ INTENTIONS

A young man from the Netherlands told me he had been a drug addict and was walking the Camino to celebrate being clean. He was tall and wiry, and his walking pace was quite fast, with his arms churning as he strode forward. Most people on the Camino learn the hard way that you have to go at your own pace. If you push it, you will tire and you will get foot/leg pain and perhaps blisters. This young man obviously had not learned that lesson.

Next to him was a very short stocky older man wearing a floppy hat that framed a pinched, ferret-like face with bushy eyebrows, long hair and a beard. He looked like a gnome. Around his neck he had binoculars. He described himself as a plant-lover. It was a quirky pair: the alleged former drug addict hyper-strider with his 'uncle' the plant-loving gnome.

I had been so confident in my gut instinct on the first half of the Camino. That confidence went out the window upon arrival in Leon, our first night of the second phase. At various places they explained that since it was a summer weekend all places were likely to be full. I had to use my cellphone to reserve a hotel, and I felt a twinge of guilt doing so, since on the first phase of the Camino it was never necessary to pull out the phone and reserve a place in advance. In the end we found a small hotel, had a filling dinner, and slept well.

We made an early start the next morning in great weather. Our destination, based on the guidebook, was Villar de Mazarife, a 21 km walk. It made sense to go easy the first day, unlike what I had done my first day months earlier back in Logroño.

The first thing I noticed about walking with my daughter was the pace. She had a quicker pace than I, and since I had learned the hard way that one should not push too much at the risk of blisters, I let her walk ahead and would meet her in the next village.

When we arrived in Villar de Mazarife it was only midday and we decided we felt strong. We stopped at a small albergue that attracted us with its nice grassy lawn where we could rest and stretch.

We refilled our water bottles and I took off my boots to massage my feet. They felt fine, but I wanted to be proactive in terms of foot care and avoid the blisters I had on the first phase of the Camino.

There was an older German couple sitting having a beer, and we saw two other women resting and eating in the shade. One of them appeared to have a foot injury.

My daughter, who at the time was in the process of being

certified to teach yoga, began to stretch and do poses. I joined her, and this became a regular part of our daily routine. What may have been a distraction for her was tonic for my tired muscles. Most importantly, we had fun doing it. She would narrate and lead me through various poses.

'Since this is our first down dog of the day,' she would begin, 'send your hips up and back, pedal your feet out, lengthen your spine, press your fingers into your mat.' Of course we had no mat, and would practice our routine in parks, a patch of grass, and – once – in a sheep meadow with the sheep looking on.

I would try my best to stretch and follow her instructions. We would usually dissolve into giggling after a short while. But she did loosen me up.

As we laughed and stretched in the sun, one of the other women joined us. It turned out she too was a yoga instructor. We later coincided with her various times over the course of the next week. She was Russian, lived in the U.S., and was traveling with her niece.

She volunteered in our first conversation that she decided to give herself '40 days on the Camino on my 40th birthday.'

She was nursing her foot on the lawn, alternatively rubbing and stretching it. She explained that while her foot was sore she had to press on.

Her companion was her 23 year-old niece, whom she inadvertently invited 'when the devil stole her tongue' during a telephone call explaining her birthday plans.

She said she loved the Camino and valued the people and adventures she had had. It gradually emerged that she had three teenage children, and had gone through a very painful divorce a year ago.

◆ ASTORGA

Astorga is an ancient town with Roman roots, remarkable churches and a bishop's palace designed by the architect Gaudi. It is also a historic center for chocolate, and while the factory was closed the day we visited, we saw they offered classes in 'interpreting chocolate.'

I asked a local for directions, and he responded by saying he had just delivered a letter to Galician President Feijoo. He asked if I wanted a copy. I said no, but he showed me the folder he was carrying, which had a letter and attached press clippings of the visit of Fidel Castro to Galicia in the 1970s. 'He's bad news!' the man said, 'this Castro guy.' I said I knew.

Later that afternoon my daughter and I were doing our stretching in a small grassy park, and noticed some older people wearing hospital gowns. We learned there was an old folks home there, perhaps explaining where the Castro letter-writer came from.

I think we were doing abbreviated sun salutations and lunges, stretching out my stiff lower back, as they watched. It must have seemed awfully strange to them. We ignored our audience.

A fellow pilgrim recommended I try the 'cocido maregato,' the local specialty. The Maregato culture refers to the Berbers who settled in the area during the time of Muslim domination, and they converted to Christianity and stayed instead of leaving in the 1300s during the Reconquest. The dish itself is unremarkable in substance but totally remarkable for its serving size and for the fact that it is served backwards. It begins with a plate full of seven different local meats including ham, different parts of the pig (ear, foot), sausage (chorizo), goat and beef. The second plate is cabbage with garbanzo beans and mixed vegetables.

Last is a noodle soup. It is an enormous dish, even for the two of us to share, and is so heavy one has to walk afterwards to begin the digestion process. Fortunately we were doing lots of walking.

✺ INTENTIONS

At an albergue in Castrojeriz we had a communal dinner of paella and salad. The meal was unremarkable but the camaraderie was not. There were perhaps 25 people at a long picnic-style table. I had a 67 year-old Englishman next to me who was quite talkative, and he introduced me to his group of fellow travelers, four couples in all. The group had done two weeks on the Camino last year and planned to do another two weeks this year.

My new friend Ian's role was to drive a beat-up VW van carrying everyone's backpacks and extra luggage to the next stop. He also made sure they had reservations for eight at the next stop.

I chatted with Ian and his group, and they were overwhelmingly positive. Each one was beaming, happy to be back on the Camino this year. Their enthusiasm was infectious.

The next morning I packed up my things and headed outside to put on my boots. It was normal practice for the albergues to keep everyone's boots in a separate area from the sleeping area, mainly to avoid the smell.

As I put on my boots another pilgrim sat next to me to put on his boots. I hadn't seen him at dinner the night before, but then again I had been distracted with Ian and his group.

Robin introduced himself. He was Canadian, and said 'call me Rob.' Rob and I left together and walked, talking, for a good while. Rob was open and talkative covering basic pilgrim banter – injuries, where did he start, how far was he going, etc.

When I asked why chose to do the Camino, he said he just needed to get away. I didn't pry, since like many people he obviously didn't want to expand on the subject.

I told him about my intentions, how my daughter had hurt herself and delayed her trip, etc., and gradually Rob started to open up. He used to be a diplomat and retired as a fairly senior guy it seemed from his description of his jobs. After retirement he and his wife divorced. He moved from the capital Ottawa, to Vancouver. I thought to myself he couldn't have gone any further away, in Canada anyway. And now he was walking between medieval villages in the middle of nowhere in Spain.

Rob said he had a few girlfriends in the years since his divorce, but as soon as the women would really commit to him he seemed to lose interest.

I told him that nobody really wants to be alone. He quickly responded that he remarried a woman ten years his junior, and within a month or two knew it was a mistake. They divorced, and although they remain friends he confessed 'I had no idea what I was doing.' He felt he should be married, and once it was done he doubted himself.

He said, 'I want to be alone. I want to do what I want to do, when I want to do it, travel, eat out, everything.'

I told him I thought it sounded like he had become hostile towards women. He said no, he still enjoys female company and goes on dates, but he has no illusions about nurturing any sustained relationship.

Our discussion was relaxed and I sensed Rob was being a little more open. We walked into a village and I ran into my Spanish friends at a café. At that point Rob said he would carry on, while I stopped to share coffee and conversation with the Spaniards.

I hoped to meet Rob again, but one never knew on the

Camino if you would run into someone constantly or never see them again. As luck had it, two days later I saw him sitting on the grass outside an albergue in Grañon. He was relaxing, alone, massaging his feet with his boots off, and it was about 4 pm, so I knew he had finished for the day, and done his pilgrim routine already.

I did my routine of bathing and washing clothes before heading outside in the sun. I found Rob, and we went to a café to get a glass of wine.

It quickly became apparent, however, that he wasn't going to return to the subjects we discussed a few days earlier. He resorted to 'guy talk' and kept our discussion at a superficial level. He insisted on paying for the wine and then excused himself, saying he needed to rest.

I'm no psychologist but I'd say Rob was really lonely, and hadn't really sorted out his feelings towards his divorce or perhaps towards women in general.

I never saw Rob again, so I don't know if he finished the Camino or not. I hope he did, and I hope he had plenty of time to think.

◆ FONCEBADON

As my daughter and I walked west from Astorga the architecture slowly changed along with the foliage. We started noticing stone houses instead of wooden ones, with smaller fenced areas on hillsides for sheep or cows. The cows were herded down the same rural roads where we walked, so one had to keep the head down to avoid stepping in cow pies. We joked that we had probably seen every cow in Spain, and – due to the ubiquitous cow pies – certainly had become acquainted with every fly.

Foncebadon is literally at the end of the road. The road peters out into just a dirt track, and most of the buildings are in ruins. There are two albergues facing each other near the top of the hill. Our intuition guided us to the one on the right, which turned out to be the right choice.

Our albergue had small rooms, highly prized by pilgrims. There were only six bunks and we shared a bathroom. The entire room was women except for me. The Asian woman, who was American, was not communicative and always seemed to be in bed, though she was actively using her cellphone or iPad. Two German women shared the other bunk. We saw them numerous times over the following days. They spoke no English (unusual for Germans) and were perfectly pleasant. I have to say they did take an inordinate amount of time in the bathroom, spiking their hair in sort of a casual rock star way, which I found absurd in the no-fuss pilgrim world. It seemed absurd to wear make-up or devote any serious time to grooming.

I did feel some sympathy for the ladies, however, since they had to endure my snoring. I complained about other snorers during my first phase on the Camino. Then, traveling with my daughter, I was informed that my snoring was keeping other people awake. I didn't want to be 'that guy,' but it turns out I am 'that guy.' Oh well. I told her she could love me for other reasons.

We shared dinner across the way with a new German friend who introduced herself as Ally. She produced a bottle of Rioja Crianza before dinner, which the three of us enjoyed immensely. Ally was from former East Germany, has two grown sons, and also had gone through a divorce. She gave an evasive response to the question of 'why the Camino,' which was typical since many people either don't know or don't want to go into the gory details.

Ally had shipped her pack to Foncebadon, and once we saw

its contents we understood why: she was carrying the bottle of wine, a bottle of vodka, and tons of creams and lotions. Her bag weighed 14 kilos, i.e. 30 lbs. Mine, by contrast, was 14 lbs. at the beginning of the Camino and 12 at the end. I wouldn't last very long carrying 30 lbs. all day long.

My daughter pointed out that Ally had really made herself up for dinner, which is highly unusual among the women on the Camino. I mean, most of us, men and women, probably look like a ragtag United Nations of homeless people walking through these tiny hamlets. I think practicality outweighs vanity for most women on the Camino: fewer creams, lotions and make up meant less weight to carry.

We did not see Ally again until we reached Santiago. There, one evening as we returned to our hotel from dinner, we saw Ally sitting on a doorstep. She said she was waiting for her 'Texan friend.' We greeted each other like long-lost best friends, and after a few pleasantries said we would see each other later. We noticed she had made herself up again, and she also had a bottle of wine to share. My theory is that Ally was looking for a hook-up on the Camino, and I hope she found it.

After dinner my daughter and I had a glass of wine in the bar and as we prepared to leave to our rooms there was a commotion. A herd of cows was coming. Pilgrims at our albergue as well as the one across the street flattened themselves against the walls as the cows rumbled through. That's an occupational hazard you don't face at most bars.

◆ CRUZ DE FERRO

The next morning we were up early and left in the dark, as was our habit, and slowly picked our way up the path from the ruins of Foncebadon. My daughter, who was leading, stopped suddenly in her tracks and started backing up. There was a herd of sheep blocking the road, and at least two goats were eyeing her suspiciously. I led her through the herd, and then realized I had left my socks on the laundry line to dry the night before. I had to return to the albergue. It was only a couple of hundred yards in distance, but it meant picking my way back through the herd. I found my socks, still damp of course in the early morning dew. I learned never to leave things on the line overnight in that part of Spain due to the humidity. Socks never dried.

I walked back through the herd again and my daughter and I resumed our trek uphill to the Cruz de Ferro, the Iron Cross where for a millennium pilgrims have left mementos, a stone, an object symbolizing leaving one's troubles behind.

We climbed the Cruz de Ferro in the dark, using our cellphones to see the inscriptions, photos and prayers left by thousands upon thousands of pilgrims. My daughter and I had each brought small stones with us, which we deposited on the pile with thousands of others. There were pictures of loved ones, hospital wristbands, handwritten notes, slips of paper with names, and all sorts of mementos. A silver object caught my eye: a packet of Ibuprofen, easily the most popular item among pilgrims on the Camino. We affectionately referred to it as 'vitamin I.' I buried a rosary among the objects, saying a prayer.

◆ THE LAST TEMPLAR

Just down the road from the Cruz de Ferro was Manjarrin, where there is a tiny albergue run by Tomas, who fancies himself the Last Templar. His ramshackle hutch is full of junk. Though still early, perhaps 7 o'clock, we found him awake, and he invited us in to his lair for coffee and biscuits. Tomas is a wonderfully eccentric guy, and in short order we solved the world's problems, from terrorism to Catalan secession.

'The Templars still exist, you know,' he said. 'They're back in the Middle East again, and they're not just playing the guitar. They're fighting, just as we always have.'

Tomas was very excited to share his political opinions. Once he got off that topic I asked how he came to Manjarrin. He said he had done the Camino many years ago and was living and working in Madrid. His life was empty, he said, so he quit his job, and returned to northern Spain to find his destiny. He lived in the area for a few years, in the small nearby towns of Acebo and Ponferrada, and finally discovered this abandoned school in Manjarrin. The building is literally falling down, and he has propped up walls with jacks and two-by-fours. Tomas made some very basic repairs and installed a wood-burning stove. He said he has lived there in that ramshackle building for years, and he remains year-round, supporting himself solely on donations. He said pilgrims always drop in, very few in the winter, though. He said the area is covered in snow, and the Camino is slippery and dangerous at that time of year. The few pilgrims he gets in the winter tend to be Koreans, for unknown reasons. Tomas is 73 years old, and one of the Camino's prominent personalities.

◈ ACEBO

The sun was up by the time we left Tomas, and we headed downhill on a steep track to Acebo. Tomas recommended we stick to the road since the path was too steep and rocky, and too many people got hurt. We did so, and it worked out, but it was a dangerous road full of sharp curves and no shoulders. Fortunately there was almost no traffic at that early hour.

We probably walked much further on the road, with all the

switchbacks, than people did on the path. We finally reached Acebo, another postcard-pretty stone village. We were hungry, and stopped in a nice bar with outdoor seating. Two different women came into the bar with injuries, one with a swollen eye and the other with a split lip. Both had slipped and fallen on the steep descent into Acebo. The one with a split lip, a Dutch woman, explained that she was more worried about the abrasions on her hands, since she was a physical therapist.

The bar was entirely made of stone, and offered different fare from what we had seen in the other regions of Spain along the Camino. The cuisine was different every 100 kms or so, from the distinctive Basque and Navarre pintxos to the wines of La Rioja, to the cheese and morcilla (blood sausage) of Burgos. Although we had not yet crossed into Galicia, in Acebo we tasted our first Galician empanadas. Unlike the empanadas in Latin America – a popover containing meat or cheese typically – these are more of a flat pastry on a cookie sheet, usually filled with cod, tuna, or chicken. The hostess at the bar cut us each a generous slice of fresh hot Galician empanada – it hit the spot and fueled us for the next few hours.

◆ MOLINASECA

We walked on another 8 kms to Molinaseca, another postcard pretty medieval village with a Roman bridge. We stopped briefly and saw many other pilgrims in outdoor cafes drinking beers, obviously done for the day. We wanted to go another 7 or 8 kms to Ponferrada, so we stopped briefly at a small restaurant on the west side of town and had lunch.

A nice couple brought us the 'pilgrim lunch,' which did not vary much from place to place, and usually offered pasta and some pork or beef. My daughter and I watched as a group of young people at another table got to know each other. There were four Italians and an American woman, all in their 20s, and all of whom we were to see almost daily for the rest of our Camino.

At one point the Italians asked the American about the brand of her jacket, which had the Patagonia logo. The Europeans were not familiar with the brand.

'Patagonia is a good brand, a good company. They have good products and they practice sustainability,' the American explained.

'I know. I'm from Seattle and I do a lot of hiking,' she added. 'I'm a piano teacher.'

◆ PONFERRADA

We took the path out of town, leading us through vineyards – we were now in the Bierzo wine region – and passing through fields of fresh blueberries, pears, and tomatoes.

We reached Ponferrada, which felt like one of the larger towns, compared to the medieval hamlets we had walked through since leaving Leon. We decided to book a small hotel right off the main square, and for a change actually looked forward to some sightseeing.

Ponferrada has a number of churches and a fully restored Templar castle. We visited the Templar church (Santa Maria la Encina), with its distinctive Templar crosses, and saw the Iglesia de Santo Tomas de las Ollas, which was built on top of a mosque. The arches inside the church showed the Arab influence, the Mudejar style one sees so often in Andalucía – Sevilla, Cordoba, and Granada.

From the castle walls we watched the local firemen combat a blaze on the mountainside facing the town. Helicopter after helicopter picked up water from the river and then dumped it over the fire. A passerby said this was a common sight due to the late summer drought.

◆ VILLAFRANCA

The terrain leaving Ponferrada became steeper and rockier. We walked over 18 miles to another beautiful town, Villafranca del Bierzo. On the way into town we passed the Church of Santiago (Iglesia de Santiago) with its famous 'Puerta del Perdon,' the 'door of pardoning.' In medieval times pilgrims who were too sick to continue to Santiago could walk through this door and receive all the same indulgences from the priests.

Villafranca is located on a hill, and its winding streets are ancient. One of them, Calle de Agua, has coats of arms on each house in lieu of numbers or addresses. We selected a small albergue along this street, and it proved to be one of the highlights of our Camino. Maria, her sisters, and her mother ran the albergue. They were originally from Ponferrada but once their sister died of a brain tumor in her 30s, they decided to renovate the grandmother's old stone home in Villafranca and convert it into an albergue. It was beautifully restored with nice wooden floors and probably the nicest bathrooms we had seen in an albergue.

We washed clothes by hand, and Maria took it on herself to dry them in her machine and left the clothes folded on my bed. I offered to pay her but she refused payment. She said she makes enough money to break even on costs; the profit she measures in the experiences she has meeting interesting pilgrims.

Maria recommended a local restaurant for a late lunch. We went to 'El Padrino' and had a wonderful meal, better than the usual pilgrim fare and still at a good price. We were the only pilgrims there. There was a large group of middle-aged diners, all of them wearing yellow t-shirts that had the distinctive scallop shell of the Camino. My instinct was to be critical of these obvious non-pilgrims, until I found the group was raising money to cure heart disease. The group sponsors walkers to raise funds. They don't pretend to be pilgrims. We later encountered other such groups funding efforts against various illnesses.

Maria recommended the Pilgrim Mass, so my daughter and I attended. Like many of these masses, it was presided over by a very old priest, and for half an hour beforehand a group of older women chanted the Marian prayers aloud, each one seemingly trying to say it faster than the other. As with all the pilgrim masses I wondered how much the pilgrims got out of it, since very few of them speak Spanish. But the priest was very gracious, and at the end of the Mass gave a pilgrim blessing along with a smile.

Back in Maria's albergue there were three of four rooms with bunk beds, five bunks per room. In the early evening our American-Russian friend and her niece showed up, our friends from the first day leaving Leon. Tagging along with her and her niece was an Italian friend, whose snoring is far worse than mine (I have witnesses!). That night I took a sleep aid (which my daughter had been carrying to cope with my snoring) and used my earplugs, and finally fell asleep at some point.

If it weren't for the snoring, I would have enjoyed spending a couple of days at that albergue in Villafranca.

❧ LA PRADELA

The guidebook sometimes offers an alternative route along the Camino. After a few days of walking, virtually every pilgrim takes the shortest route possible, no questions asked. So as we left Maria's beautiful albergue in the dark the next morning, we had an option to continue on a relatively flat path along the shoulder of a road, or a steeper prettier mountain route 1.5 km longer. We chose the latter.

They say the Camino only gives you problems you can handle. That path turned out to be steeper, rockier, and much much longer than the flat route. We did not regret it, however, since we came across a tiny albergue with only a few beds in a hamlet called La Pradela. The hostess made us ham and eggs with fresh squeezed orange juice. She and her German assistant Angela – who seemed to stare at us as if they don't see many pilgrims – could not have been nicer. She showed us her stamp she uses to stamp the pilgrim credential, explaining that an American couple that stayed there devised the design and made the stamp for her.

We spent a nice half hour with them – and with their cat Mimo and their dog Tua – before parting as friends. It was one of those Camino experiences where in a very short period of time you feel a real kinship with someone or some place. If it weren't still morning, I would have enjoyed staying overnight there. With any luck no snorers would arrive and I could get a good night's sleep.

We then followed the path onto a road and down, curving switchback by switchback, back to the main road. We calculated first that our route was way more than 1.5 km longer, and second, although our friends from Villafranca were by now well ahead of us, we didn't care.

❖ LAGUNA DE CASTILLA

We walked a total of 21 miles that day, and perhaps more due to our detour across the mountain to La Pradela. We went through Cacabelos and made a stop at a tiny restaurant in Pieros. A lovely older woman hosted us. We asked if she had any croquettes (croquetas) and she proceeded to make them from scratch. It took a little longer than we expected but meanwhile she gave us a slice of crab and ham tortilla. We stopped for coffee and snack, and ended up getting a gourmet meal. She was quite a cook, and a very nice lady.

Our hostess back in La Pradela told us about a great little albergue in Laguna de Castilla, which was not the recommended stopping point in my guidebook. She was right: since it was a small place I called ahead to ask them to hold two bunks until at least 3 pm, which they did.

The recommended stop was La Faba, which made sense because it was at the foot of the steep climb to O Cebriero. Better to do the climb first thing in the morning. We went further, about halfway up the infamous climb, and stopped, exhausted, at her friend's place in Laguna de Castilla.

As we walked up to the nondescript albergue there was a small crowd of dirty pilgrims waiting outside. I shuddered to think it might be full. The prospect of continuing the climb was not an option. I worked my way inside and said I had called, and they honored it. We got the last two bunks available. I don't know if it helped that that their former schoolmate from La Pradela had recommended us. We were happy to take off our packs that day.

The highlight at this albergue was the little restaurant. We enjoyed a beer after our long hot day, and saw the Asian-American woman again, along with the two German ladies. An Aussie stopped by for some conversation, but since he couldn't get a room he was going to have to continue up the steep hill to O Cebreiro.

Again, as at Foncebadon, that night we had a herd of cows run right through the street as pilgrims were lounging outside, sending us all scurrying for cover. Apparently the cows are a natural hazard in Galicia.

✦ O CEBREIRO

We were up and walking in the dark, as usual, slowly making our way up the steep path to O Cebreiro. We departed around 6:30 am, and reached the top as the sun was just emerging. It was an ethereal scene, a barren countryside shrouded in mist. You could only see 30 or 40 yards in any direction, and at the crossroads at the top of the hill we stood for a few minutes looking for the correct route, no yellow arrows or scallop shell markers in sight. Other pilgrims emerged out of the gloom and we followed them on what turned out to be the correct route into the tiny village of O Cebreiro.

The town is all stone and very picturesque. At its center is the church, which is beautiful in its simplicity. Significantly, it contains what it claims is the Holy Grail. The chalice is encased in a silver case donated by the Queen of England. The church is well known among pilgrims since it is the highest point on the Camino, so pilgrims like to pray there. In addition, the couple I had met from San Diego, California way back in Santo Domingo, months earlier, decided to get married on the Camino and did it in that church.

A small chapel in the church contains the grave of the priest who did more than anyone to make the Camino accessible. Pilgrims frequently got lost in the area in the 1970s and 80s, and used to constantly ask Father Elias Valiña Sampedro for directions. It occurred to him that he could put the pilgrims on the right track and at the same time popularize the Camino. He had some extra yellow paint on hand, so he traveled up and down the Camino in Galicia painting the yellow arrows we see at intersections.

Outside the church was an effigy of Santiago. Upon inspection I saw that if you inserted a one-euro coin and a 50-centime coin then it would imprint a St. James coin for you. I had a one-euro coin but neither my daughter nor I had a 50-centime coin. We asked at a couple of stores, with no luck. We went into a café/bar that was downstairs in a basement. I took off my pack and as I placed it behind my table I saw a coin on the floor: a 50-centime coin. What were the chances? I gave it to my daughter, who went outside to the Santiago coin machine, and…it didn't work. It had been broken for a long time, the proprietor told me.

The proprietor served us fresh tortillas and bread with a large steaming café con leche that was most welcome after the long, cold climb. We hated to leave the warm café. We noticed some tour buses, the first I had seen for awhile. Some pilgrims start their Camino at O Cebreiro.

We mustered our courage and made our way through the early morning downhill. The path started winding through lush green valleys and through forests of chestnuts. All around you could hear the sound of chestnuts dropping on the ground. I was waiting for one to hit me in the head.

We stopped at a little café two hours later to have our first caldo gallego, the well-known Galician soup made of turnip greens with white beans. It was delicious, especially in that cold humid climate. With the long climb early that morning, we were now in Galicia, the mountainous, rainy northwest corner of Spain. The countryside was lush and green, and the evenings and early mornings were cold. The cuisine changed, and in this region seafood and white wine are prized.

✿ THE TRUE PILGRIM

As we got closer to Santiago, we had the option to take a detour to Samos, the famous monastery. We chose not to, but I made a mental note that on a future Camino I would like to not only see Samos but also stay overnight there, since they offer pilgrims a Mass along with a bunk.

The route once again was along paths with cathedral ceilings of chestnut trees. We saw horses and sheep in the fields. Galicia was quite a contrast to the flat, hot Meseta.

The most significant part of this day's trek was passing through Sarria, a popular place for pilgrims to join the Camino since they are almost precisely at the 100km marker from Santiago. Pilgrims have to walk at least 100 kilometers to earn their certificate (known as a 'compostela') testifying they had completed the Camino.

We saw tour buses disgorging streams of hikers with new REI equipment and little daypacks. The main impact, though, was the noise: they were loud, and constantly laughing. I noticed the Americans, since I pick up on the accent, but there were tourists from a wide variety of countries getting off those buses.

While Sarria has many albergues and restaurants, due to the influx of people on the Camino, we chose to keep walking to Barbadelo. We stayed in a very small out of the way house converted into an albergue. We had it to ourselves, I thought, until we had showered and rested, at which time others started filing in. We knew virtually all of them: the group of five young

Germans we had seen repeatedly, the four Italians who now knew all about Patagonia brand clothing, and a Colombian.

There was a nice open field next to the albergue, so my daughter again began giving me instruction. 'Bend over and stretch out your hamstrings. Let your arms hang and rag doll. Lift your knee to your waist; now open it to the outside, like the hinge on a fence. Now the other knee. Lift your arms over your head, now twist right, then left.' We did the low lunge, and really stretched out the hips and legs. The stretching got the blood flowing, and relieved soreness in the legs.

Half a kilometer down the road was the official Barbadelo albergue, which looked nice and had a very good restaurant. We went there for dinner, again sampled the caldo gallego and had some fish, the Galician specialty.

Since we were now nearing Santiago de Compostela, we paid more attention to our daily mileage and gauged that we could arrive comfortably within three or four more days. That realization was sobering, since after walking so far it gave the indication that the Camino would soon be over.

We estimated we would have to cover 22 miles that day in order to make Santiago in three more days. We used our cell-phones as flashlights for the first hour or two, and saw relatively few people, even after our first stop for coffee and a tortilla. It wasn't until about 9 or 9:30am that the new pilgrims, who had been unloaded at Sarria, were up and about and on the Camino. From about 9am on, every café and restaurant had many more people, and every hotel was fairly full. Albergues would be fine, since these 'pilgrims' didn't stay in albergues: their travel agents booked them in the best hotels.

Whereas almost all the pilgrims earlier on the Camino walked with their backpacks, we noticed that those starting at Sarria had only daypacks.

Were these transgressions violations of The Pilgrim Code? I didn't feel this was very pilgrim-esque, if there is such a word, though I kept telling myself to accept them and not be judgmental.

The problem was I saw these fresh healthy bodies bound from tourist buses, wearing brightly colored clothing and smiles. Most notably, they were clean; they even smelled clean.

It was hard not to hate them.

Thinking about the newly minted pilgrims made me think 'what is a true pilgrim?' I had this notion of a Code of the Pilgrim that felt somehow violated.

I thought about that many times a day during my Camino. Is the person who stays in Paradors, the state-subsidized historic sites converted into luxury hotels, and has his backpack or luggage shipped ahead every day less of a pilgrim? What about the pilgrim who decides to take the bus instead of walking the last 10 kms into Burgos? Does stepping into any type of vehicle or transportation automatically disqualify you?

And what about those who do the Camino in stages, as so many do--are they lesser pilgrims than those who cross the Pyrenees? My first thoughts were to measure the 'degree of pilgrim-ness' in a person by how much they had suffered. If you have walked the entire Camino from France you have suffered. I saw a person pushing his paralyzed brother in a wheelchair on the Camino. Surely he will receive special indulgences in Heaven.

JAN

I remember Jan, a Dutchman, who I had met along the Camino. He started his journey back in Holland, traveling to the Spanish border to begin his trek. He said he spent six weeks walking from Holland to St. Jean, and he didn't care how long it would take to finish the Camino. So before even beginning at St. Jean, he had already walked much farther than the 500 mile Camino.

Asked when he expected to finish, he said it didn't matter. Once he got to Santiago he planned to go south to Fatima, Portugal, since it was the 100th anniversary of the appearance of Mary to some children in that town.

Jan rolled his own cigarettes and picked bits of tobacco from his lips as he spoke. His fingertips were stained yellowish orange from nicotine.

I noticed the crucifix around his neck and complimented him on it. He said he had made it himself, carving it from wood. He then produced a rosary from his pocket, and said he recited Marian prayers while he walked the Camino. He said every day he would see new things, and each time he saw something unique or beautiful he would pull out his rosary and recite a prayer of thanks.

Jan and I shared a communal meal in a church on the Camino, and started conversing as we helped gather plates and clean up. We then went outside and continued talking.

Jan had been traveling along the entire route from the French border. Asked about his feet and his physical well being, he said he had blisters on his blisters and was fine. He obviously enjoyed some level of suffering, or at least wanted to appear that way.

He explained that when one is alone, one is focused on the pain and the blisters. When you join up with other pilgrims along the route, start up conversations and start to learn the reasons others embark on their journeys, you tend to stop focusing on yourself and you lose sight of the pain. Sharing with others keeps you going, keeps you from dwelling on your personal problems.

Jan said that the suffering and pain is the same in real life. He said he gets more satisfaction because he has been alone and suffered. He knows he can get through it and so he is more eager to help others.

'We need to suffer, don't we?' he asked.

I thought about what Jan said for days afterward, and I decided that some suffering – within reason – was probably necessary in order to break through one's mental barriers and achieve true growth. We don't need to go barefoot like monks in medieval times, but the blisters and the physical wear and tear help you realize you can stay committed to something and reach your goal despite physical pain.

In many conversations with other pilgrims we discussed what I call the Code of the True Pilgrim. The True Pilgrim walks; it is a 'Camino,' from the Spanish verb 'caminar,' i.e. to walk. Lesser people stayed in Paradors, or had their pack shipped ahead, or took taxis. Among other pilgrims those people were tourists, not pilgrims, 'touregrinos' as opposed to 'peregrinos.'

At the same time, I knew I shouldn't judge, and that all of us were venting out of pain or because we had walked more miles than others. Feeling superior to others is not a pilgrim trait. Judging is not a pilgrim trait. Pilgrims accept others and accept their circumstances, and never regard others are somehow lesser.

Others do the Camino by bicycle. The minimum distance required to get a compostela by bike is 200km. The cyclists are sometimes on our Camino path and sometimes on the roads, since they can't really navigate the paths, especially the steep ones (for example to the Cruz de Ferro or to O Cebreiro).

Like those using hiking poles, cyclists are annoying due to their lack of what I would call pilgrim etiquette. They don't yell 'on your left' as they do in the U.S. to warn you they intend to pass. Pilgrims walk on the paths and do not tend to stay to the right. And the cyclists will pass you as easily and suddenly on the right as on the left. I have seen uncharacteristic pilgrim anger as a cyclist narrowly misses them on the path without so much as a by your leave.

So I tried mightily to convince myself not to hate both the tourists with daypacks and the cyclists.

◆ HUMILITY

Despite my best efforts, I had one unfortunate run-in with a 'touregrino.' My daughter and I arrived in Arca, the second-to-last stage of the Camino, 20kms short of Santiago, after walking ten hours. It had been a particularly exhausting day. Our mileage for the day was about 22.5 miles according to the guidebook, but as if that weren't far enough, that only got us to the town of Arca. It was another 4-5 kilometers to our hotel. We were tired, it was hot. I waited to check in behind a well-dressed, clean American man in his 50s. He turned to me to make conversation and asked 'Have a nice walk today?' 'No,' I snapped. I immediately regretted it. He then said he had had an easy day, walking from Arzua, which had been our midday stop. I realized he was a day packer, had walked less than half what we had, but I had no business reacting in such an 'unpligrimesque' way. I felt ashamed, and thought about it for days afterwards. I had violated the Pilgrim Code.

At first I had the same negative judgmental reaction to people using technology. Surely technology was a violation of the Code. It actually bothered me to see pilgrims constantly taking GPS readings instead of following the yellow painted arrows and scallop shell markings. It also bothered me to see people walking along the Roman Road of the Meseta, only to find they had in ear buds and were probably listening to heavy metal.

I realized over time that I had to temper my mental accusations. One of the heavy cellphone and GPS users, I found out, was in fact directing a drone overhead filming the Camino. And another person with ear buds, I discovered was listening to a recording of her mother's voice. I admit to occasionally using my cellphone to reserve a room at an albergue or hotel, so I really could not cast stones. I became more humble.

Some of the people I met and the stories you hear on the Camino also taught me the value of humility. Whatever my ill-defined reasons for being on the Camino, I heard about the 70 year-old man leading his blind wife on the Camino, narrating everything he was seeing. That was powerful.

I also heard from another pilgrim that he met an older man walking alone, who said his grandson was terminally ill. Along the Camino he prayed for God to take him. He did not want to see his grandson die, and preferred to die first so he could greet him in Heaven.

It was hard not to be humbled by the passion and commitment of these pilgrims.

Of course there are some nutballs on the Camino as well. I have already told the story of the time I met 'Father Joy,' the fake priest who came up with his 'Joyfulness Church of St. Christ' while in prison for assaulting his wife. No big deal, just blasphemy.

I also heard about a transvestite pilgrim who wore a short, tight pink dress with her (his) hiking boots, and carried a stuffed tiger in her arms.

I saw other pilgrims who I sometimes thought were beggars. Perhaps they had been on the Camino so long that it was a way of life, depending on gifts from others to eat.

There were others, throwbacks to the hippie era, who had done the Camino and then returned and set up a stand offering fruit and bread in return for a donation. At least twice during the Camino I would turn a corner on a remote path and find a guy sitting casually strumming a guitar. One of them, outside Rio Orbigo, looked to me like a gypsy. They just want a euro for a song, but I think they misjudge the audience: they believe all foreigners are wealthy, when this particular group of foreigners is living on a very humble budget.

❖ BAG OF FEARS

While we started seeing clean people walking quickly with no backpacks starting at Sarria, we also met one woman outside Portomarin who was visibly suffering due to a knee problem. She said she had been walking for weeks and her knee pain was getting worse. She would not give up. Her solution had evolved from carrying her backpack to shipping it ahead, in order to lighten her load. She also changed tactics: she was staying in hotels now to get better rest, and every day would shuffle along as far as she could, and then take a taxi back to her hotel. The next day she would take a taxi to her furthest point of advancement and begin walking again. She would then change hotels to the next town. A true pilgrim, or a misguided person who was risking serious injury?

In the little town of Morgade we came across a gem of an albergue. It was another low stone building, and the ladies running the albergue welcomed us inside into the warmth, where we enjoyed fresh farm eggs and homemade sausage.

When we had walked 21.5 miles we decided to stop in Hospital Alta da Cruz at a rural hotel. Over dinner we met an American woman and her Italian male friend Marco. Suzan and Marco had met along the Camino and both had started back at St. Jean. She told some funny stories about being locked in various bathrooms along the Camino, and said she had learned to use reverse psychology when things got hard. For example when facing a steep hill she would put in her ear buds and 'climb the hills dancing.'

Suzan also described her backpack as her 'bag of fears,' referring the things one thought they couldn't live without. Her strategy throughout the Camino was to ship her 'bag of fears' forward to the next stop, since she wanted to lighten the load and reduce the chance of an injury. At the same time by adopting this strategy she had figured out clearly what she could live without. She said that list included make-up, shampoo, extra shirts and pants, among other things. She had also devised many shortcuts; for example she stopped washing her socks. Since they are pure wool, she said, they take forever to dry. (I was guilty, as many other pilgrims are, of hanging my socks off my pack so they would dry while I walked.) Suzan said one should just air them out; washing them required 24 hours of drying time, which we don't have.

Suzan raised an interesting point about pilgrims needing to 'give back' since they had learned valuable lessons about themselves and others. She said she felt a responsibility to do something with the knowledge she had gained on the Camino.

She also said she fully intended to swim naked off the coast of Finisterre upon completing it.

◆ OCTOPUS

It was a long walk the next day to Melide, known as the world's capital for octopus. It is a small city or large town, and we arrived tired and hungry, so after locating our hostel and showering/changing, we charged right back out to find the highly recommended Ezequiel Restaurant. We ordered the 'pulpo al feira,' which is disks of fresh grilled octopus topped with paprika. We watched the cook scooping small octopi out of a large copper vat of boiling water, and then snipping the tentacles into bite-sized disks. The octopus is best accompanied by the local Ribeiro white wine, with some baked cod and a salad on the side. We ate like barbarians.

Our longest walk was to Arca the next day. It was 22.5 miles to Arca and then another mile or two to the hotel. By this point, our second to last stop, we had to book places in advance due to the high number of pilgrims in every town as we neared Santiago. It took us ten hours, much longer than normal. Our pace was a bit slower, and we had some stops, notably for some fresh local cheese in Arzua, topped with honey. The anchovies we ate may have caused my daughter some stomach distress, and that may have delayed us a bit as well. It was a long day.

Fortunately we knew just how to deal with it. After showering and changing clothes, we lay on the beds with our legs vertical up the wall. 'Dad, it's time for an inversion. Let the blood flow out of your legs. Give your feet a break. Now, slowly inhale, bring your knees to your chest, grabbing the inner or outer sides of your feet, and gently pull your knees down. Rock back and forth, massaging the lower back.' This was the 'happy baby pose,' properly known as 'Ananda Balasana.' Needless to say, every time we did the 'baby pose' we broke up laughing, and that loosened me up and raised my spirits more than the yoga pose itself did.

❧ SANTIAGO

We deliberately pushed ourselves the day before so that we would have a relatively short walk the next morning into Santiago. As it worked out, by 9am we passed Monte de Gozo (the so-called 'hill of joy' from where pilgrims can first see Santiago's church spires in the distance), all the while picking up more pilgrims from every direction. We walked 13 miles to the city limits of Santiago. From there it was about 40 more minutes into the Plaza and the cathedral.

We went straight to the Plaza del Obradoiro, the famous square with the cathedral containing the remains of St. James. The cathedral itself was mostly covered in scaffolding. Pilgrims lay about the plaza, talking in groups, napping, and greeting arrivals as long-lost friends.

My daughter and I treated ourselves by reserving a room at the beautiful Reyes Catolicos Parador right on the square. Queen Isabella and King Ferdinand commissioned the building as a hospital to take care of pilgrims, back in the 15th century. The building has been beautifully restored into perhaps Spain's most luxurious parador.

In medieval times pilgrims were frequently robbed by highwaymen, or succumbed to disease or illness, or even attacks from other pilgrims. They were in sorry shape arriving in Santiago.

The royal order and funds from Ferdinand and Isabella provided for three days of lodging and medical attention in summer, five days in winter. The hospital staff also included priests, so the pilgrims' souls as well as their bodies were healed.

The hospital also had a famous fire in the 17th century that killed many pilgrims. So it occurred to me that this luxurious resting place for pilgrims was also the place where perhaps more pilgrims had died than anywhere else.

The hotel is part of Spain's chain of paradors. In the 1950s and 1960s General Franco commissioned a study of Spain's extensive patrimony of historic buildings, many of which were in ruins. Many of the most historic castles, monasteries, and churches were designated 'paradors' and were renovated to accommodate guests.

Some of Spain's most luxurious hotels are paradors. This list would include the Reyes Católicos as well as the San Marco in Leon.

Once we were shown our room, we emptied our backpacks, took off our boots, and spent some time checking out the bathroom, which was larger than most places we had slept for the past two weeks. It also had a bathtub! I spied the basket with toiletries and immediately thought of which ones I could take with me.

We showered and changed and then went to the Pilgrim Office to stand in line for almost two hours to obtain our compostelas. One pilgrim was showing companions his compostela. It was a beautiful medieval style scroll, written in Latin with the name of the pilgrim inserted in stylish calligraphy. I made a mental note to frame mine and hang it in a prominent place in my home. While in line we ran across friends and spotted other familiar faces from along our route. It was old-home week. We realized we could probably spot friends and acquaintances for days if we remained there.

◆ SPIRITUAL OR RELIGIOUS?

When it was my time to present my passport and pilgrim credential to the official in the Pilgrim Office, the young man politely asked for my passport and my pilgrim passport, with stamps from each albergue where I had stayed. He then inquired if I had walked the entire way. Yes, I said. Then he asked if my intention was religious or spiritual. I hesitated. I told him it was both, and as I said it I felt it was more than that. Were those my only two choices? Even though I had spent weeks dwelling on the subject multiple times per day, once confronted I felt I needed more time to sort out my answer. So why did I do the Camino?

◆ PILGRIM MASS

We went to various pilgrim masses along the Camino, but Santiago's was by far the most impressive and the most meaningful. The main difference is the cathedral itself, which is one of Spain's most impressive gothic cathedrals (along with Burgos and Leon).

There are so many tourists at the Santiago Pilgrim Mass that the clerics make a series of multilingual announcements before Mass asking that all those not attending should leave by the side doors. But again most pilgrims – and most tourists – don't understand Spanish or the hard to hear announcements, and jam the aisles.

The Mass itself was wonderful. The readings were about faith and thankfulness. It was tailored to the pilgrims, whose journey was all about faith and who were very thankful to have completed their journey.

The priest's homily was about the Gospel we heard from Matthew. The passage was the well-known one that asks (paraphrasing) 'who of you, if your son asked for bread, would give him a stone; and which of you, if your son asked for fish, would give him a snake?'

The priest explained that the pilgrims had endured all manner of inconveniences, pain and suffering along the

Camino. But they had learned through each other that they could overcome their suffering and keep moving toward their goal. What the pilgrim had learned, he explained, was a lesson in faith that they could apply to their real Camino, i.e. their personal life. 'For everyone who asks receives; he who seeks finds; and to him who knocks, the door will be opened.'

The highlight of the Mass for many of the visitors was the pendulum swinging of the silver incenser (the 'botafumeiro') back and forth across the nave of the cathedral, symbolically lifting the congregation's prayers up to heaven.

Despite the priest's admonition that the pilgrim's journey was not ending but rather just beginning, the Mass was a wonderful way to finish the Camino.

We celebrated by going to eat at a recommended small restaurant and enjoyed a paella-like dish of saffron-flavored rice filled with shrimp, clams, and mussels, accompanied by a bottle of local Albariño wine.

We then returned to our luxurious room and slept nine hours, undisturbed by any rustling and snoring from pilgrims along the Camino.

◆ FINAL THOUGHTS

One American couple I met had just finished their third Camino. In addition, they had done the Portuguese Camino, a two-week trek from Lisbon north to Santiago de Compostela. They were in their 50s, and they told me they did two pilgrimages per year. The reason: they love the people they meet along the way. They said they love their neighborhood in Colorado, but they prefer to meet the random international pilgrims along the Camino. 'Everyone appears to be happy, and they want to help each other,' they said.

I noticed the husband was wearing a Tau cross around his neck. I asked if his reasons for undertaking the Camino were religious. No, he said, he wore the cross mainly so others would know he was a fellow pilgrim, as I had when we started talking.

I remembered going through the town of San Anton earlier on the Camino that tau crosses decorated the 13th century hospital there, which was named for St. Anthony, the Egyptian monk who was later venerated as a saint.

The cross is also identified with St. Francis of Assisi, who himself did the northern route ('Camino del Norte') of the Camino in the 13th century. The Franciscan Order today uses the tau cross as one of its symbols.

Later on I thought about what the American couple had said. The Camino is a wonderful experience that helps the pilgrim to find out about himself through long periods of silence and introspection, and through dealing with pain. The solidarity with other pilgrims is important: it helps carry you forward and gives you faith.

But it seemed these people preferred the alternative reality of the Camino to their personal lives. Of course it is easier to live on the Camino, where life is simplified and there are few responsibilities and even fewer material possessions and modern-day distractions.

◆ AMERICAN PILGRIM

We met an American as we waited in line in Santiago at the Pilgrim Welcome Center. He had walked the full Camino from Saint Jean, the French border. He was lanky and his t-shirt had holes on each shoulder, just where a backpack would rub. He obviously hadn't shaved in a few days, but he had a peaceful expression and was quick to smile and engage.

Asked by other friends what he would do now that he was finished in Santiago, he said he would just start walking west, toward Finisterre, 'to see what happens.' He said he didn't know how far he would go or how long. He added that he was hungry but did not want to stay and eat; instead, he had some carrots left over from yesterday in his pack, and he'd be ok.

The American's response reminded me that – just like the American couple we had met – some people found it easier to be a pilgrim than to navigate real life with daily chores, routines, and responsibilities. Many pilgrims were 'recidivists,' i.e. they had done multiple Caminos. I can understand the desire to return to Spain and do one of the various Caminos to Santiago, learning more about oneself. But it is not a substitute for reality, an alternative or escape from the world.

◆ WHY?

I asked myself that question multiple times a day. And pilgrims ask each other the same question. No pilgrim really cares what you do or what your profession is/was. After exchanging information on each other's foot ailments, the subject pretty quickly gets to why you are on the Camino.

The Camino is like a confessional in the sense that you tend to open up very quickly to people you have never seen and probably will never see again. You share hardship and fears and anxieties with these people, so you feel an instant kinship even if you have never spoken to each other. I could see a pilgrim three or four times over two weeks, and if we glimpsed each other on the street in Burgos or Leon we would meet like long-lost friends, although we had never spoken to each other. Why?

There are people of all ages: groups of young people, talking and laughing as they walk; older people, some who have done the Camino multiple times; sick people, even dying people. I recalled coming across the marker of the English priest who came to the Camino to die. People recovering from a divorce, a medical procedure, a bad relationship, a family tragedy, or people who want to take a personal inventory of their life.

The statistics are eloquent. In the early 1980s only 5,000 people a year did the Camino. By the year 2000 over 100,000 completed the journey, and by 2012 200,000 did. By the end of September 2017, only 15,000 were needed to break the 300,000 mark.

Of these, approximately 56% were men, 44% women. Spaniards made up about half of the pilgrims, with 50%, followed by Germans, Italians, and other Europeans. Americans made up 3.6% (as of 2012).

Of the total, the majority (20%) started at Sarria, with 100 km to Santiago. The next most popular point of departure was St. Jean Pied de Port, with about 11%. These statistics are soft, since the totals are based on those obtaining a compostela in Santiago. I can imagine a number of serious pilgrims were more interested in the experience than in the certificate. In addition, many others join in the Camino for a week one year, another week a year later, and don't obtain their certificate.

This is a self-selected group. Why don't they hang out on a beach, travel to Machu Picchu or trek the Himalayas? Why a pilgrimage?

Most pilgrims are quite open about why they are on the Camino. It may take a few conversations to get beyond the superficial first answers, but there are usually profound reasons for undertaking such an arduous journey. You see them taking the experience seriously, writing in journals, sitting alone with their thoughts.

I don't believe most pilgrims are religious. Some clearly are. But many, especially the younger ones, although probably not raised going to church or catechism, are searching for meaning. With churches locked all over Europe amid a widespread secular movement, it is understandable that people want to understand who they are and why they are alive. Some young people told me they weren't religious but they believed in justice, tolerance, peace, and protecting the environment. They said they weren't spiritual but they were drawn to the Camino. Some attended the pilgrim Masses offered at churches in the small towns along the way. I can't fully understand that since most of them didn't speak Spanish, but it was clear that they were curious, and they were searching for meaning.

I'd guess that many were at a crossroads in their life, had gone through a divorce or a family tragedy, or had survived a life-threatening medical procedure. Of course those were not the reasons they typically gave for going on the Camino. Some were just tourists. But you could sense a seriousness about many pilgrims that was deeper than the flip response given.

◆ WHAT DID I LEARN ON THE CAMINO?

Once I returned to the U.S., I explained to a friend that I had just completed the Camino, and she asked me point blank: so what did you learn on your pilgrimage? It was a question I had thought of endlessly, but it was not easy to come up with easy answers.

I decided that the pilgrims weren't just normal people with issues and problems but were called to do this pilgrimage as a way to work things out, seek clarification or get to know themselves better. Or at least try. My first thought in response to the question 'what did I learn?' was the quality of people on the Camino. Whatever their intentions, these were interesting people.

I was always impressed with the kindness of the volunteer hospitalers at the albergues. Virtually every one had completed the Camino and wanted to support it. That reminded me of one pilgrim's admonition that, having completed the Camino, one should 'give back,' try to represent what the Camino stands for. I tried to be a 'True Pilgrim,' whatever that was, but sometimes slipped and used my cellphone or became judgmental. Along the way I encountered as many different intentions as I did people, but was impressed by the seriousness of those people. I think of Paco dedicating a Camino to God after recuperating from a brain tumor. Or the Stoicism of Juan. Or the love I witnessed, watching a 70 year-old man leading his blind wife, narrating the Camino for her.

Secondly, walking the Camino reveals the attractiveness of leading a simpler life. I know what I need to live on the Camino, so I will henceforth question the need for certain material goods. I know I don't need them in order to be happy. Of course I love some of my material goods, and prefer having them, but I'm also happy when I recognize I don't need them. Status, wealth, and success are less important now; I have simpler goals.

What is important to me is love, who I love, who loves me, and my family.

Thirdly, with Santiago almost in sight, I was ashamed at how I snapped at a fellow American, a 'touregrino' who wore a daypack and stayed in hotels. I knew better. I knew that as a 'True Pilgrim' I should not be so judgmental and in fact should be more humble. Having retired from a demanding career ten years ago, I also need to accept who I am and what I am at this stage in life.

I learned to be thankful for basic things, a welcoming host, a comfortable bed, good food, and a good night's rest.

I learned that I could set large goals and meet them, for example walking across Spain for 500 miles. I can commit to a target and attain it by breaking it down into small pieces, one day, one kilometer, one step at a time. I feel a directness of purpose I didn't have before.

We all have a 'backpack full of fears,' as Suzan said. Our fears are our burdens. If we recognize that, we can discard them, overcome them.

I learned to trust my gut instinct, my intuition. Thinking of how things could be worse puts problems into perspective, and enables me to think positively. I am more self-reliant.

I remain very thankful I got to spend two weeks with my daughter. She will probably never dedicate two weeks to the old man again, so to me the time and the experience we shared was precious. I reminded myself of the need to actively form memories with the people I love most, starting with my children. I need to start working on that.

I also have learned to love walking. As the priest said at Mass upon completing the Camino, 'enjoy the rest of your Camino,' i.e. the rest of your life is before you. I will. I continue to walk and learn, and I know I won't stop.

William Ross Newland is a world traveler and avid cook. His passion is trying to recreate his foreign culinary experiences at home in his kitchen. When he is not traveling and writing he runs The Delian Group, a consulting firm that specializes in Latin America.